SIMON &
SCHUSTER

# The One Thing
# You Need to Know

*. . . About Great Managing,*

*Great Leading, and*

*Sustained Individual Success*

## Marcus Buckingham

**SIMON &
SCHUSTER**

London · New York · Sydney · Toronto

A VIACOM COMPANY

This edition first published in Great Britain by
Simon and Schuster UK Ltd, 2005
A Viacom Company

1 3 5 7 9 10 8 6 4 2

Simon and Schuster UK Ltd
Africa House
64-78 Kingsway
London WC2B 6AH

www.simonsays.co.uk

Simon and Schuster Australia
Sydney

A CIP catalogue for this book is available from the British Library

ISBN 0-7432-6326-X
EAN 9780743263269

Printed and bound in Great Britain by
The Bath Press, Bath

*To my mentor, Don, for his wisdom and his faith.*

*To my wife, Janie, for hers.*

# Contents

Contents

## PART II

## The One Thing You Need to Know
*Sustained Individual Success*

# The One Thing
# You Need to Know

# CHAPTER 1

# A Few Things You Should Know About the "One Thing"

## "GET ME TO THE CORE"

> *"If you dig into a subject deeply enough, what do you find?"*

In one sense this book began with a conversation with Carrie Tolstedt in a hotel lobby in Los Angeles. Carrie is the head of Wells Fargo's regional banking group, a position she has held for the last four years and in which she has been inordinately successful. As with many effective leaders, though, she is by nature self-critical. Despite the fact that she had just delivered a rousing speech to her regional managers, I was not overly surprised to find her standing off by herself looking a little dissatisfied.

"What's up?" I said. "The speech went really well." One always tends to offer reassurance to speakers after a speech, but in this case it was accurate. She had been speaking on the subject of customer service and how, with most banking products being a commodity in the marketplace, Wells Fargo would live or die based on the quality of its service. This message isn't new, either for Wells Fargo or the wider business world, and in the wrong hands it can pretty quickly descend into cliché. But Carrie had managed to keep the message coherent, the stories personal, and the examples vivid and powerful. It was a good speech.

"I don't know," she replied. "Sometimes I'm not sure how effective these speeches really are. The regional managers will now try to pass the message on to their district managers, and inevitably it will get tweaked in some way, changed somehow. Then it'll get changed again when the district managers pass it on to their store managers, and again when the store supervisors hear it, until, by the time it reaches the people who can really use it—our customer service reps and personal bankers—it will be significantly altered.

"Don't get me wrong, it's good that each level of my organization adds its own spin, but still, I sometimes think that the only way to keep this organization on the same page about customer service is to boil it down to its essence. My message should be so simple and so clear that, across all forty-three thousand employees, everyone comes to know what's at the core."

At the time, I think I mumbled something about being sure that her message would get through to where it mattered most, but on a subliminal level her wish—to see a subject so clearly that she could describe its essence simply, but without oversimplification—must have registered. For weeks thereafter, no matter where I went on my travels, no matter whom I was talking to, I seemed to hear the same wish: "Get me to the heart of the matter."

Sure, the subject in question varied. Some people wanted to know the organizing principle of great management. Others were more interested in the essence of great leadership. Others asked about the driving force behind a successful career. But everywhere the wish was the same: Get me to the core.

Now, I suppose I could have chalked these wishes up to intellectual laziness. Why struggle with complex reality when you can skate by on the PowerPoint version of life instead? But this is a rather uncharitable and, in the end, unhelpful interpretation. We are all attracted to clarified versions of reality not because we are intellectually lazy, but because these versions often wind up being so useful. Take winter, spring, summer, and autumn as an example. The four seasons are the PowerPoint version of the weather. Certainly they leave out a great deal of complexity, exception, and local variation, but nonetheless they've helped generations of farmers time their sowing and harvesting.

If there were any charges of intellectual laziness to be levelled, they probably should have been levelled at me. For seventeen years I had the good fortune to work with one of the most respected research organizations in the world, the Gallup Organization. During this time, I was given the opportunity to interview some of the world's best leaders, managers, teachers, salespeople, stockbrokers, lawyers, and all manner of public servants. The fact that I hadn't isolated a few core insights at the heart of great leadership, or managing, or sustained individual success didn't mean that these insights didn't exist. It simply meant I hadn't yet been focused enough to get it done.

Carrie's wish, and the many similar wishes I heard in the months following, pushed me to get focused. Since people wanted to reach down into the heart of the matter, I was, I realized, in a perfect position to help them get there. My research experiences at Gallup mostly consisted of surveying large numbers of people in the hopes of finding broad patterns in the data. Now, in my effort to get to the core, I would use this foundation as the jumping-off point for deeper, more immersive, more individualized research. I wouldn't survey a large number of good performers. Instead I would identify one or two elite players, one or two people who, in their chosen roles and fields, had measurably, consistently, and dramatically outperformed their peers. In the end these individuals covered a wide range, from the executive who transformed a failing drug into the best-selling prescription drug in the world, the president of one of the world's largest retailers, the customer service representative who sold more than fifteen hundred Gillette deodorants in one month, the miner who hadn't suffered a single workplace injury in over fifty years, all the way to the screenwriter who penned such blockbusters as *Jurassic Park* and *Spider-Man*.

And having identified them, I planned to investigate the practical, seemingly banal details of their actions and their choices. Why did the executive turn down repeated promotions before taking on the challenge of turning around that failing drug? Why did the retail president invoke the memories of his working-class upbringing when defining his company's strategy? The deodorant-selling customer service representative works the night shift. Is this relevant to her performance? One of her hobbies is weightlifting. Odd? Yes, but can it in any way explain why she is so successful so consistently? What was each of these special people actually doing that made them so very good at their role?

I have chosen to focus this deep dive on the three roles that are the most critical if you are to achieve something significant in your life and then sustain and expand this achievement, namely the roles of manager, leader, and individual performer. In Part I of the book we focus on the two roles that underpin sustained *organizational* success.

### What is the One Thing you need to know about great managing?

To get the best performance from your people, you have to be able to execute a number of different roles very well. You have to be able to select people effectively. You have to set expectations by defining clearly the outcomes you want. You have to motivate people by focusing on their strengths and managing around their weaknesses. And, as they challenge you to help them grow, you have to learn how to steer them toward roles that truly fit them, rather than simply promoting them up the corporate ladder.

Each of these roles involves significant subtlety and complexity. But, without denying this complexity, is there one deep insight that underpins all of these roles and that all great managers keep in the top of their minds? The chapter on great managing supplies the answer.

## *What is the One Thing you need to know about great leading?*

When you study truly effective leaders, the first thing that strikes you is just how different they are. I could use any number of examples from today's business world, but instead, think back to the first four presidents of the United States. Although each of them experienced great success in rallying people toward a better future, their styles could not have been more dissimilar. George Washington's leadership style was to project an image of soundness and constancy, but he is not remembered as an inspiring visionary. In direct contrast, the second U.S. president, John Adams, *was* an inspiring visionary. He was so gifted a public speaker that he could hold a vociferous Congress in rapt silence for hours. However, as his struggles following the end of the Revolutionary War revealed, he was at his best only when railing against a perceived foe—which, most of the time, happened to be Great Britain.

His successor, Thomas Jefferson, did not require a foe to bring out the best in him. Sitting alone at his writing desk he could conjure compelling word pictures from the blank sheets in front of him—and yet, in contrast to Adams, he so feared public speaking that he changed the protocol so that all of his State of the Union addresses were written out and then handed to an assistant who ran down the street and delivered them to Congress.

James Madison was different again. He was a small man with a light voice who was unable to rely on inspiring word pictures to lead. Undeterred, he opted for a more pragmatic, political approach, working the floor of Congress and, one by one, building the alliances necessary to advance his agenda.

Despite these obvious differences and imperfections, each of these individuals is rightly upheld as a model of excellence in leadership. Thus, my question for the chapter on great leading is "When you study models of excellence in leadership—whether 250-year-old models or those of the present—can you look past the superficial idiosyncrasies and identify one primary insight that explains why they excel?"

In Part II we shift our focus to sustained *individual* success.

### What is the One Thing you need to know about sustained individual success?

During the course of your life you will inevitably be exposed to all manner of options, opportunities, and pressures. The key to sustaining success is to be able to filter all these possibilities and fasten on to those few that will allow you to express the best of yourself. But what filter should you use? Should you actively seek out experiences that will enable you to acquire a broad range of expertise, so that you have something to fall back on when one expertise becomes obsolete? Should you stick with a role that doesn't suit you, thereby proving to your superiors that you are a good soldier, willing to play any role for the benefit of the team? Should you imagine that your career has distinct stages and that the filter used in the early stages should be replaced with new ones as your career progresses? Or does it all depend on what kind of career you have chosen, or even what kind of personality you have?

In chapters 5, 6, and 7, we come to grips with these questions and reveal the one insight you must never forget as you strive for sustained individual success.

## A LIFETIME OF "WHY"S

*"What drove this book?"*

Before we get started, a word about myself. We're going to be in each other's company for the next few hours (days? plane rides?), so you should probably know whom you're dealing with. Although in one sense I owe the impetus for this book to my conversation with Carrie Tolstedt, in another sense, it was almost inevitable that at some point in my life I would sit down to write this book.

I always found the movie *City Slickers* a little disappointing. It wasn't that I didn't enjoy it—the story of three stuck-in-a-rut New Yorkers heading out to a dude ranch in the American West to learn about life and friendship and loyalty is charming, and Billy Crystal, the lead, is as hysterical as ever. No, what always bothered me about the movie was that it teases the viewer and then fails to deliver on its tease. About thirty minutes into the movie, Billy's character is trying to engage the ranch's trail boss, played by Jack Palance as a stone-faced loner, in a debate about the meaning of life. Disdainful of Billy's frenetic city-boy prattle, Palance's character, Curly, turns in the saddle to face him and holds up one finger.

"I'll tell you the secret to life. This one thing. Just this one thing. You stick to that and everything else don't mean s——."

"What's the one thing?" Billy's character asks.

"That's what you've got to figure out," Curly replies.

Since this answer didn't satisfy me, I sat through the entire movie in the hope of learning what the one thing really was. It wasn't a good sign when Curly died about an hour in, but still I stuck with it, confident that a sentimental Hollywood film would never set me up so blatantly and then fail to follow through on the punch line. But it did. At the end of the movie, when Billy and his two chums are standing on the mountain top, pondering their recent daring, their life lessons learned, and Curly, the philosopher–trail boss, Billy announces that he now sees clearly the path ahead of him.

"Why?" asks one chum.

"Because I know what he meant."

"Who?"

"Curly." Billy holds up one finger. "I know what he meant by this."

"What?"

Billy then proceeds to say exactly what Curly had said an hour earlier: "That's what you've got to figure out."

"I'm gonna deck you," says his friend.

Well, my thought exactly.

"That's what you've got to figure out." What kind of an answer is that? I was holding out for something deep and meaningful and, above all, short, some pithy little phrase that I could quote around the water cooler the next day, something like Bogart's line in *Casablanca,* "The problems of three little people don't amount to a hill of beans in this crazy world." Or Laurence Fishburne's in *The Matrix,* "Welcome to the desert of real" (said very slowly). I would even have settled for something akin to Ali MacGraw's "Love means never having to say you're sorry." But no, all *City Slickers* could give me was "That's what you've got to figure out."

I suppose I have only myself to blame for expecting a summer blockbuster to deliver some deep truth, but, to be honest, I have always been attracted to the notion that beneath complex phenomena such as loyalty, or productivity, or career success, or even happy marriage, you can discover a core concept. And that armed with this core concept, you can focus your attention, see the causes more clearly, and so waste less time, be precise, make accurate predictions, and act with precision to make these predictions come true. The very idea that these core concepts exist, and can be discovered, is thrilling to me.

Many of my most vivid memories stem from the discovery of a core concept that, all by itself, served to clarify something that, a moment before, had seemed unfathomably, ineffably complex.

I remember sitting in chapel one morning—all good English public school boys started their day in chapel—and hearing 1 Corinthians 13:13 for the first time: "And now faith, hope, and love, abide these three; and the greatest of these is love."

I didn't fully understand its import then, and perhaps I still don't, but I can recall being terribly excited that Saint Paul had done the analysis and concluded that, while all three were great, love was the greatest.

Since then my pantheon of certifiably cool concepts has grown. Some were deemed cool simply because they applied to me personally. From the time I was about three until just after my twelfth birthday I was cursed with a terrible stammer. Along with being hugely embarrassing, it was also, on the days when I was feeling rational enough to ponder it, intellectually perplexing. Why did I stammer? Why couldn't I say my name without drawing it out into a mess of staccato consonants and bizarrely elongated vowels? I knew my name well enough. I could even sing my name on cue. I just couldn't utter it in normal conversation. There was no rational explanation for my stammer, no identifiable cause, and as a result it became, to my young mind, more powerful and dangerous.

And then, in a magazine picked up in a doctor's waiting room, I happened to read that boys who had been exposed to higher than normal levels of testosterone in the womb were more likely to develop autism, dyslexia, and, believe it or not, stammering. The physical manifestation of this overdose of testosterone, I read, was that the boy's ring finger would be significantly longer than his index finger. Upon reading this, I immediately looked down at my fingers and noticed, I think for the first time, that my ring finger extended far beyond my index finger, almost matching my middle finger in length.

I can remember being deeply happy with this discovery. My stammer had a cause. It was, in some small way, predictable, understandable. I could start to get my mind around it and therefore, perhaps, control it. Coincidence or not, a couple of days after discovering the cause of my stammer, I felt it slipping away. Today it's virtually gone, sneaking up only occasionally, when I'm overtired or overstressed.

Some concepts were deemed cool because they were so wildly unlikely as to be just plain silly. The fact that the tides are caused by the pull of the moon falls into this category. When my brother first told me this, I thought he was pulling my leg, like the times he persuaded me that whales laid eggs or that moths raised their young in streetlights and flew around them all night to keep them warm. But, upon further investigation, I discovered that, however improbable it sounded, my brother's explanation was correct: the moon, hanging small and distant in the night sky, somehow caused the sea to sweep up the beach and swamp my sand castles, and then pulled it back out again.

Other concepts were deemed cool because they managed to explain so much so simply. In this category falls my all-time favourite concept: natural selection. Every time I think of it I am floored that someone (more accurately two people, Charles Darwin and Alfred Russel Wallace) was perceptive enough to pierce nature's indescribable variety and identify the mechanism that created it. A concept that has the range to explain why eyes develop, why male sea horses give birth, why all human anger is caused by self-righteousness, why birds fly south for the winter, and most every other living form and function, and with such economy that even an eighth grader can grasp it, is surely the king of concepts. When he read about it in an early copy of *On the Origin of Species,* Darwin's friend T. H. Huxley was reported to have said what many of us have probably felt at one time or another: "How stupid of me not to have thought of it." Amen to that.

Don't misunderstand. I am not so naïve as to believe that you can reduce all complex phenomena to a single cause. In fact, as a social science researcher by training, I have been forced to become singularly suspicious of oversimplifications, the kind that lead to one-size-fits-all explanations and get-slim-quick-pill action plans. No matter how careful your analysis, the link between the effect you are trying to predict and the factor you thought was causing it never turns out to be quite as clear and direct as you had hoped.

If you have a statistical mind-set you will be familiar with the frustrations. First, the correlation between the cause and the effect is never very strong. Positive correlations range from 0.0, no correlation whatsoever, all the way to 1.0, a perfect, positive correlation. In the social sciences, if you discover a correlation of a mere 0.5 you swoon with happiness. For example, although you'd make a lot of money betting that taller people weigh more than shorter people, the correlation between height (the cause) and weight (the effect) is only 0.5.

And second, even when you discover a positive correlation between two factors, you can rarely be certain which is causing which, or indeed whether a third, entirely different factor is causing both. For example, if you analyzed the link between BMW drivers and laptop owners you would find a positive correlation between the two, but obviously buying a BMW doesn't cause you to rush out and buy a laptop, or vice versa. Both can best be explained, and thus predicted, by something else, in this case level of income and education.

So yes, I have become sceptical of oversimplification. But this scepticism hasn't dampened my desire to dive to the bottom of a subject. Nor has it stopped me from believing that if one digs into a subject carefully enough, one can dredge up, beneath the surface complexity and unpredictability, a few deep and deeply useful truths.

## THE TESTS FOR THE "ONE THING"

*"Why are some explanations more powerful than others?"*

"Controlling insights" rather than "deep truths" is, I think, a better way to describe what we are after. "Controlling insights" conveys the sense that although they do not explain all out-comes or events, they do serve as the *best* explanation of the *most* events. Other factors will undoubtedly come into play, but the kinds of insights that are most useful are the ones that under-pin, and that therefore control, every other factor. These insights give you leverage. They help you know which of your actions will have the most far-reaching influence in virtually every situation.

In fact, for a concept to emerge as the controlling insight, as the One Thing, this is the first test it must pass: *It must apply across a wide range of situations.* Take leadership as an example. Lately, much has been made of the notion that there is no one best way to lead and that, instead, the most effective leadership style will be determined by the situation in which you happen to find yourself. Winston Churchill is usually wheeled out as the best proof of this. During the peaceful interwar years his belligerent, confrontational style was so ineffective that he was pushed out into the political wilderness, but this very same style proved extraordinarily effective when the situation changed and he was called upon to stiffen Britain's resolve against the Nazi assault.

There's no doubt that different situations do require different actions from the leader, but this doesn't mean that great leadership lacks a One Thing. Nor does it mean that the most deeply insightful thing you can say about leadership is that it's situational. This is surely a bit of a cop-out. Instead, as we'll see in the chapter on great leading, with enough focus and precision you can identify the controlling insight that explains great leading across all situations, all styles.

The second test is this: *The controlling insight must serve as the multiplier.* It must explain excellence in a particular arena, not average, not mere survival. In any equation some factors will have only an additive value—when you focus your actions on these factors you see some incremental improvement in the outcomes you want. The controlling insight should be more powerful. It should show you how to get *exponential* improvement. It should point to where you will net the greatest return on the investment of your time and energy.

For example, many factors combine to produce good managing. However, if you look closely, you'll quickly see that most of them don't turn talented employees into superstar performers. They merely ensure that you don't end up discouraging your employees to such an extent that they quit, either physically or psychologically. Don't pick people with no talent for the role. Don't set unclear expectations. Don't say you'll do one thing and then do another. Don't ignore them when they excel. Don't keep such a distance that you fail to build a relationship with them. Don't play them off against one another. Don't ridicule their ideas. Avoid all of these behaviours and, of course, you will be less likely to chase your best people away.

However, none of them survives as the One Thing you need to know about great managing, because none of them is the multiplying ingredient that elevates a manager from good to great. This is precisely what the controlling insight at the core of great managing must explain.

In short, no matter what the subject, the controlling insight should not merely get you onto the field of play. It should show you how to win and keep winning the game.

The third and final test: *The controlling insight must guide action.* I'd wager you bought this book not simply because you are curious and inquisitive, but rather because you want to get better at something. You want to *do* things differently, not simply look at them differently. To help you, the controlling insight must lead to action. It must point to precise things you can do to create better outcomes more efficiently and more consistently.

So, these are our three criteria for identifying the controlling insight, the One Thing: it must apply across a wide range of situations, it must serve as the multiplying factor that elevates average to excellent, and it must lead to more precise actions. To show you what we're after, here is one controlling insight that survived these tests and that should prove helpful in your personal life. Initially, this example might seem like a protracted digression. I chose to include it, though, not only because it survived the three tests, but also because it was so clearly derived from careful studies of excellence.

## ONE CONTROLLING INSIGHT

> *"What is the One Thing you need to know about happy marriage?"*

You might think that social science makes a habit of studying excellence in order to learn about excellence, but it really doesn't. For the last hundred years or so, the prevailing wisdom was that good is the opposite of bad, and so in order to understand good, one should study bad and then invert the findings. Thus depression and neurosis were studied in order to learn about joy. Children on drugs were studied in order to learn how to keep children off drugs. Truants were studied in order to figure out how to keep kids in school. And unhappy marriages were studied in order to help the rest of us know how to avoid divorce.

Unsurprisingly, these studies revealed that, in unhappy marriages, neither partner understood the other very well—they couldn't identify accurately the other's strengths, weaknesses, or values. Consequently, guided by the prevailing assumption that good must be the opposite of bad, the advice to couples in marriage therapy became, Love may be blind, but a strong relationship should not be. In a strong relationship, a clear-eyed assessment of your partner's strengths, weaknesses, and values should, over time, replace the initial rush of love. So listen to your partner. Understand that she may see the world differently from you. Love her for her strengths, but then identify, accept, and offer support in her areas of weakness. Together a perfect whole will be forged from your two imperfect halves.

On its face, this advice—replace love blindness with an accurate understanding of who your partner really is—seems sensible. If you understand your wife accurately, she will feel more understood and therefore more secure. On the flip side, if you expect her to possess strengths that in fact she lacks, you will surely clash when she surprises you with her behaviour. Even worse, if you cling to an idealized version of her, sooner or later she will fail to live up to it, and your fragile relationship, built on an illusion, will crack and break.

From many angles, this advice seems to hold water.

However, over the last two decades, the focus of investigation has shifted away from bad marriages. Under the impetus of the leaders of the school of positive psychology—Martin Seligman, Donald O. Clifton, Mihaly Csikszentmihalyi, Ed Diener—the prevailing wisdom has come to incorporate the idea that good is not the opposite of bad, merely different, and that if you really want to identify the distinct characteristics of great marriages you must study the great ones with as much discipline and rigour as had previously been brought to bear on the bad ones. If you can discover what lies at the core of these great marriages, and offer advice stemming from these discoveries, you are much more likely to help people build lastingly rewarding partnerships.

Researchers from the State University of New York at Buffalo, the Universities of Michigan, British Columbia, and Waterloo, and Sussex University have opted for this approach, and their findings directly challenge the conventional wisdom that a happy marriage is founded on clear-eyed understanding and acceptance of each other. In its place they have identified a defining characteristic of happy marriages. This characteristic is so deeply counterintuitive that initially most of us will have difficulty absorbing it. And yet, upon reflection, it may just lead us to the controlling insight at the heart of a happy marriage.

These researchers have interviewed thousands of happily married or cohabiting couples over the course of many different studies, but for our purposes, I'll focus on the one that first caught my eye. In this particular study Dr. Sandra Murray, a soft-spoken professor from SUNY Buffalo, and her colleagues began by asking 105 couples (77 were married and 28 were cohabiting) to rate each other on a list of qualities, such as "kind and affectionate", "open and disclosing", "tolerant and accepting", "patient", "warm", and "sociable". They then asked the couples to rate how rewarding and satisfying they found their relationship. These couples were not love-blind honeymooners, but couples of long standing. The average length of the relationship was 10.9 years.

(A quick note: from this point on I am going to write from the perspective of the husband rating his wife. This will make things easier for me and, I hope, more comprehensible for you as I attempt to explain the findings. If you don't feel like digging up the actual research paper, you'll have to trust me when I tell you that everything I am about to describe holds true whether the husband is rating the wife or the wife the husband. If you do feel like digging up the paper, it is titled "What the Motivated Mind Sees" and can be found in the *Journal of Experimental Social Psychology,* volume 36, pp. 600–620.)

If it were true that accurate understanding of your partner is crucial to the building of a strong relationship, when a husband rates his wife high on "patient", "warm", and "sociable" but lower on "open and disclosing" and his wife rates herself in the same way, they should be a very happy couple. Put more simply, when their pattern of ratings match, their level of satisfaction with the marriage should be high.

Apparently not. A match between the husband's ratings of his wife and the wife's ratings of herself showed no correlation whatsoever to how happy they were in their relationship. I'm not saying there was a negative correlation. Accurate understanding of each other's strengths and weaknesses did not make the couple *more* dissatisfied. There was simply no correlation, no observable link between accurate understanding and marital satisfaction.

However, one distinct pattern did emerge. In the happiest couples, the husband rated the wife more positively than she did on *every single quality.* For some reason, the husband in a highly rewarding relationship consistently credited his wife with qualities that she didn't think she had.

A cynic might label the husband's ratings delusions. If my wife doesn't think she possesses these qualities but, after ten years, I still do, then perhaps "delusion" is not too strong a word. The researchers opted for more measured terms, such as "positive illusions" and "benevolent distortions" and "idealizations", but, whatever the label, there was no mistaking the conclusion: in the happiest couples, the husband stays blind.

Now, you might still wonder whether the happy husband, blinded by his positive illusions, is heading for a fall. My wife and I may be happy today, but woe betide us both when my wife fails to behave in line with my expectations.

The same thought occurred to the researchers, and so they decided to track these couples over the next few years. What did they find? The husband who rated his wife high on qualities that she didn't think she had was not only more satisfied with the relationship today, but in the months following reported even greater levels of satisfaction, fewer sources of conflict, and fewer moments of doubt.

So there you have it. The husband who assumes that his wife possesses strengths even she doesn't think she possesses will have a strong marriage today and an even stronger one tomorrow.

I must admit that when I first encountered this finding, it seemed through-the-looking-glass bizarre to me, as it may to you. Accurate understanding of each other doesn't lead to a stronger relationship? How can this be true? Each of the studies confirming this finding has been published in a refereed academic journal, so I trusted that it was in fact true. But *why* was it true?

This is how the researchers begin their explanation:

> Few decisions have higher stakes than the decision to commit to one particular romantic partner. In perhaps no other context do adults voluntarily tie their hopes and goals to the good will of another. To feel happy and secure in the face of such vulnerability, individuals need to believe that their relationship really is a good one and that their partner can be counted on to be caring and responsive across time and situations.

When I tie myself to my wife, I am making one of the biggest commitments of my life. To avoid cognitive dissonance, I make myself believe that the commitment I made is a good one. My problem is that my wife is not perfect, nor does she see the world in exactly the way I do. If I dwell on these imperfections and differences of perspective, I will become insecure about my decision and, soon, about my safety in the relationship itself. As a result, I will be less comfortable with real intimacy, less forgiving, less positive in my judgments of her, and things will slowly fall apart.

So, instead, I *overstate* the case for my commitment. I come to believe that my wife has more strengths than she actually thinks she has. These perceptions may not be real, in the sense that they may not reflect what my wife is really like. But, nonetheless, they serve the needs of our relationship very well. They make me feel secure in my decision, secure in my relationship, and therefore, even in moments of extreme vulnerability, my trust in the relationship trumps my need for self-preservation. Because I am fortified by my positive illusions, when my wife does something that upsets me, I will not retreat and look for ways to get back at her (not often; not deliberately; at least, not often deliberately) but instead will reach toward her for greater intimacy.

And so, over time, my positive illusions create an upward spiral of love. My illusions give me conviction. My conviction leads to security. My security fosters intimacy. And my intimacy reinforces love.

Putting these conclusions together, this controlling insight can serve as the One Thing you need to know about happy marriage:

**Find the most generous explanation for each other's behaviour and believe it.**

Love begins with positive illusions, but in strong marriages, these positive illusions do not give way to a dispassionately accurate understanding of each other's strengths and weaknesses. Instead these positive illusions weave their strength into the fabric of the relationship, until they actually become the relationship. They make themselves come true. Stated more bluntly, your positive illusions will make your love last.

As with all controlling insights, this One Thing should help you act with greater precision as you strive to strengthen your relationship. For example, the researchers tell us that when you notice a flaw in your spouse, you should not compartmentalize it. Do not put a line around it, give it a name, set if off to one side, and then try to balance it out with her positive traits, as in "Yes, she is a short-tempered person, but, on the positive side, she is also caring and creative." Balancing out clearly delineated weaknesses with equally clearly delineated strengths may seem sensible but, unfortunately, it won't help your relationship. The research reveals that husbands and wives who do this to each other end up with more doubts, more conflicts, and less rewarding relationships. It's almost as if, by defining your spouse's weaknesses specifically and vividly, you imbue those weaknesses with unwarranted power. They may lurk off in the wings for a while, but, like a stage villain, they are primed to leap out of the shadows at any moment and ruin the fun.

Instead, the researchers tell us, when you notice a flaw, recast it in your mind as an aspect of a strength. Thus "She's not impatient, she's intense." Or "She's not narrow-minded, she's focused." Initially this may feel like you're playing mind games with yourself, but you're actually doing something quite clever. Remember: the strongest relationships over time are those in which each partner finds a way to build on his/her idealized image of the other. By recasting weaknesses as aspects of a strength you are integrating all available information into this idealized image. Thus your idealized image is stronger and more robust because no new information, no newly discovered flaw, can undermine it. Any new flaw is simply reformatted as a thread of a strength, and then woven right back into your idealized image.

As I said, this insight runs counter to the conventional wisdom on marriage and may be difficult for you to square with your view of your own relationship. Does this mean you shouldn't try to understand your spouse? Does this mean you and your spouse should never argue? What happens if your positive illusions keep getting undermined by the fact that you and your spouse value things that are diametrically opposed?

The answers to these questions could probably fill a whole book, and since this isn't that book, I won't dwell on them now. Nonetheless, despite these questions, I chose to include this recent finding on happy marriage because it was so clearly the result of a rigorous study of excellence. At the very least it should make you stop and think about how you are choosing to perceive your spouse. As the research reveals, your perceptions not only colour your current reality, they actually alter your relationship and thereby create your future reality.

And if you worry that all this is derived from some new-fangled study that subsequent research will probably refute, here is the eighteenth century poet William Blake saying pretty much the same thing and reminding us that there really is nothing new under the sun:

Man's desires are limited by his perceptions; none can desire what he has not perceived.

So, when looking at your spouse, choose your perceptions with care. They will fuel your desire.

. . .

At this point, let's leave the mysteries of marriage behind and return to the three questions at the heart of the book. What is the One Thing you need to know about

- Great managing
- Great leading
- Sustained individual success

Each of these subjects is rich and complex. Each could be explored endlessly to detail fully their many facets. My aim in this book is not to deny the complexity of these subjects, but to penetrate it; not to make these subjects simpler, merely clearer. After all, we live in a world of excess access. We can find whatever we want, whenever we want it, as soon as we want it. This can be wonderfully helpful if we are trying to track down last month's sales data, an errant bank statement, or a misplaced mother-in-law, but if we are not careful, this instant, constant access can overwhelm us.

To thrive in this world will require of us a new skill. Not drive, not sheer intelligence, not creativity, but focus. The word "focus" has two primary meanings. It can refer either to your ability to sort through many factors and identify those that are most critical—to be able to focus well is to be able to filter well. Or it can refer to your ability to bring sustained pressure to bear once you've identified these factors—this is the laser-like quality of focus. The skill targeted by this book incorporates both of these meanings.

Today you must excel at filtering the world. You must be able to cut through the clutter and zero in on the emotions or facts or events that really matter. You must learn to distinguish between what is merely important and what is imperative. You must learn to place less value on all that you can remember and more on those few things that you must never forget.

But you must also learn the discipline of applying yourself with laser-like precision. As we will see, the common thread running through each of the three controlling insights is that success, whether as a manager, a leader, or an individual performer, does not come to those who aspire to well-roundedness, breadth, and balance. The reverse is true. Success comes most readily to those who reject balance, who instead pursue strategies that are intentionally imbalanced. This focus, this willingness to apply disproportionate pressure in a few selected areas of your working life, won't leave you brittle and narrow. Counterintuitively, this kind of lopsided focus actually increases your capacity and fuels your resilience.

My hope for this book is that it will arm you with the insights you need to sharpen both aspects of your focus, the filter and the laser, and thereby enable you to manage, lead, and perform with extreme precision and effect.

PART I

# The One Thing
# You Need to Know

*SUSTAINED*
*ORGANIZATIONAL*
*SUCCESS*

# CHAPTER 2

# Managing and Leading: What's the Difference?

## A VITAL DISTINCTION

> *"Are they different? Are they both important?*
> *Can you do both?"*

After writing a book about great managers, *First, Break All the Rules,* I imagined that when companies asked me to speak to their employees they would want me to talk about that subject. Strangely, they didn't. Almost without exception they wanted me to talk about great leaders.

Everyone is fascinated by leadership. An organization may possess great products, great processes, great customers, and great employees, but apparently without great leaders their future is bleak. Leadership, people would have you think, is the secret sauce that, when ladled liberally over the whole organization, will lead to innovation, initiative, "intrepreneurship", and creativity.

And there are all kinds of leadership recipes on offer. Visit your local bookshop and you will discover books such as *Primal Leadership, Authentic Leadership, Servant Leadership,* or, if you're feeling a little more adventurous, *Leadership Secrets of Attila the Hun, Leadership Jazz, Shakespeare on Leadership,* and my current favourite, *Leadership Sopranos Style.*

We wouldn't have this plethora of books if the demand weren't so strong, and the reason for this demand is that leadership is not reserved for leaders. On the contrary, the conventional wisdom seems to be that each employee is, or should be, a leader. To quote Michael Useem, director of the Center for Leadership and Change Management at the Wharton School, "Everybody should be good at leading, whatever their level in the hierarchy."

And conveniently, the conventional wisdom also holds not only that everyone should be a leader, but that everyone *can* be a leader. Leaders, apparently, are not born, but rather are made by their training and their diligence. Here is one of many possible quotes on the subject, this one from the authors of *Primal Leadership:* "The challenge of mastering leadership is a skill like any other, such as improving your golf game or learning to play slide guitar. Anyone who has the will and the motivation can get better at leading, once he understands the steps."

As far as I can tell, only two business experts have cast doubt on leadership as the ultimate panacea: Jim Collins and

Peter Drucker. Collins, in his book *Built to Last,* observed that the most sustainably successful companies relied less on leaders than on organization-wide phenomena such as cultlike cultures and core ideologies. Although I and many others found his arguments persuasive, he obviously still nursed some sympathy for the leader-as-saviour storyline. In his next book, *Good to Great,* based on his study of eleven companies that had dramatically improved their performance, Collins describes himself succumbing to the pressure of his research team: "Early in the project I kept insisting, 'Ignore the executives.' But the research team kept pushing back. 'No, there is something consistently unusual about them. We can't ignore them.' "

Inevitably, this unusual "something" turned out to be leadership, albeit a special kind, which Collins and his team came to call Level 5 Leadership. Level 5 leaders are not your celebrity-seeking, ego-driven types, but rather are characterized by their quiet assurance as they push steadily and resolutely toward their goal. In Collins's words, they "build enduring greatness through a paradoxical blend of personal humility and professional will." These Level 5 leaders are, in his new scheme, one of the key ingredients in the recipe for transforming a company from good to great.

This leaves Drucker as the lone holdout. He by no means dismisses leadership as a powerful force. On the contrary, he believes that the leader's role is critical to the organization's sustained success. "The leader," he writes in *Managing for the Future,* "sets the goals, sets the priorities, and sets and maintains the standards." Where he differs from everyone else is that he refuses to make a distinction between effective management and effective leadership. He uses the following story to make his point.

A certain vice president of human resources once called him up to ask him to give a lecture to her company's employees on charismatic leadership. He described to her the chief responsibilities of an effective leader and then, he writes, "After I had said these things on the phone to the bank's human-resources VP, there was a long silence. Finally she said, 'But that's no different from what we have known for years are the requirements of being an effective manager.' 'Precisely,' I replied."

Where do I stand in this ongoing debate about the role of the leader and the role of the manager? Well, fortunately, since I hold in high regard each of the people I've just quoted, I share their basic premise that great organizations require great leaders. In all of the studies of organizational excellence in which I have participated, excellence was impossible to explain without factoring in the role of the leader. Naturally, the importance of the leadership role varies according to the type of challenge the organization is facing—when the organization is confronted by dramatic change, the guiding hand of a strong leader is more influential than when the organization needs simply to maintain its current course. But, in general, my experience conforms with that of Warren Bennis, perhaps the preeminent leadership expert, when he says, "Leadership accounts for, at the very least, 15 percent of the success of any organization."

However, apart from agreement on that basic point, I must confess that my research contradicts pretty much everything else. First, Drucker's overarching genius notwithstanding, is he really right on the subject of leadership and management? Yes, they are both critically important to the ongoing success of an organization, but no, they are not interchangeable. On the contrary, the role of the leader and the role of the manager are utterly different. The responsibilities are different. The starting points are different. The talents required to excel at each are different. And, as we'll see, the One Thing you need to know about one is not only different, but is, in fact, the exact opposite of the One Thing you need to know about the other. This doesn't mean that you cannot excel at both. You can. But it does mean that, if you want to excel at both, or if you want to choose between one or the other as your primary focus, you need to be aware of the difference.

Second, it is inaccurate and not a little unhelpful to say that everyone, regardless of his or her place in the hierarchy, must be a leader. Leaders play a distinct, discrete, and enormously difficult role within an organization. If everyone is trying to play leader, they will lose focus on their primary role—whether it be sales, or service, or design, or analysis, or management—and quite quickly the organization will splinter apart.

Third, because leadership requires certain natural talents, the notion that anyone can learn to be a great leader, no matter how appealing it is at first glance, is equally inaccurate and unhelpful. The same can be said for great managers. Obviously, you can improve your performance as either a leader or a manager through practise, experience, and training (as we'll explore in later chapters), but if you lack a few core talents you will never be able to excel consistently in either.

And finally, although I appreciate what Collins was railing against—egomaniacal leaders such as Al "Chainsaw" Dunlap,

Dennis "Shower Curtain" Kozlowski, and Jeffrey "Off Balance Sheet" Skilling—the most effective leaders are not self-effacing and humble. In fact, a powerful ego, defined as the need to stake grand claims, is one of their most defining characteristics (although, obviously, not the only one).

Given the flood of opinion to the contrary, each of these disagreements requires some explaining. We'll explore most of them later in this chapter, but let's come to grips with the first one right now. How exactly do the roles of the manager and the leader differ?

## A VIEW FROM THE MIDDLE

*"What do great managers actually do and what talents do you need to do it?"*

One of the great thrills of my job is that I get to meet people like Manjit Kaur. Manjit is a service clerk for Walgreens whom I first heard about at Walgreens' biannual convention in Las Vegas a couple of years ago. Dave Bernauer, the CEO, had asked me to speak before Walgreens' four thousand or so store managers about the challenges of building a great place to work, so one summer morning in 2003 I could be found pacing the corridors outside the cavernous meeting hall, rehearsing my opening remarks.

Twenty minutes before my speech was due to begin, as I always do, I slipped into the back of the hall to see the stage from the audience's point of view and to get a sense of how I would need to project myself in order to reach the most distant eyes and ears. In this case, there *was* no back of the hall. Four thousand people is such a large audience that Walgreens had decided to arrange the hall as you would for a boxing match: a brilliantly lit square stage in the middle, surrounded on all four sides by row upon row of exquisitely uncomfortable convention chairs.

As I was mentally choreographing when in my speech I would turn to face each quadrant, the words of the current speaker filtered in and broke my concentration. He was Walgreens' head of marketing and he seemed to be talking about some kind of sales contest.

"We have had great success," he declared, "with many of our sales initiatives. In particular I want you all to congratulate Manjit Kaur. Like all our service clerks, Manjit participated last month in a contest to see who could sell the most Gillette deodorants. The national average was three hundred units. Does anyone want to guess how many Manjit sold?"

I doubt he was expecting an answer, but he paused for a good long time, as all speakers do when they know they're armed with a zinger.

"One thousand six hundred!" he boomed. "One thousand six hundred Gillette deodorants in one month! Let's hear it for Manjit!" This last sentence was unnecessary. He was presenting to a crowd educated in the realities of retail, so the moment they heard the amazing number, they clapped, hooted, and stamped their admiration. It was a powerful convention moment.

I confess I was slightly dismayed at this reaction, because frankly, it's a lot easier to follow a speaker who has lulled the audience to sleep than one who has just electrified them.

But my curiosity was also sparked. Sixteen hundred deodorants is a lot of deodorants. Who on earth was this Manjit Kaur? How did he do it? Where does he work? Would Walgreens let me interview him to learn his secret? I was so preoccupied by these questions that I forgot my mental rehearsal about when to turn and whom to face, with the unfortunate result that I wound up giving the speech walking around and around in ever-faster circles. (I don't know why I sped up. It just seemed like the right thing to do at the time.)

Fortunately, despite my postspeech dizziness, I maintained enough presence of mind to follow up about Manjit. Could they track him down for me? Could I interview him?

The answer to both questions was yes, and three months later I walked into the windowless back office of Walgreens store 842, in San Jose, California, and met the extraordinary Manjit Kaur.

My first discovery was that Manjit is a woman. She is originally from the Punjab, in India, and immigrated to the United States with her husband three and a half years ago. She is trained as a computer technician, but since her degree is not recognized in the U.S., she currently attends the local technical college and works at Walgreens to pay her tuition.

My second and more directly relevant discovery was that Manjit did not win just one month's contest. Of the thirteen contests Walgreens has held thus far, Manjit has won six. Whether the promotional item for the month is deodorant or disposable cameras or toothpaste or batteries or low-carb candy bars, Manjit excels at selling it. Even though, like all superstars, she has spikes of peak performance—during the month she won the

Gillette deodorant contest, she sold five hundred of them in a single day—her real genius lies in her consistency.

My third and most startling discovery was that Manjit works the graveyard shift, from 12:30 p.m. to 8:30 a.m. Apparently her school schedule forces her to. I don't know about you, but if I were struggling to perform in one of these sales contests, I might use the excuse "I can't compete because I'm working the graveyard shift and don't get to meet many customers." Manjit, obviously, has no need for excuses. Despite the fact that she meets significantly fewer customers than her peers, she somehow finds a way to persuade the majority of them to buy what she is selling.

And she clearly loves what she does. Manjit's English is fluid rather than fluent. Initially, she seems shy, but ask her a question and she smiles wide as the words tumble out of her. I ask her if she will become a computer technician once she completes her degree.

"I come here, I am happy. My husband says, 'Walgreens is your store, not your home.' But I say, 'I don't care.' I come here, I am happy. I might study for pharmacy, pharmacy technician . . . maybe. Maybe. But I don't think I like it. I like my job now. Yes."

Naturally, I ask her for her secret.

"Manjit, you consistently sell over five times the national average, no matter what the product. How do you do it?"

More smiling. "I don't know. I just like it. And every customer like me. I know their name. I know everybody and everybody knows me. I walk the store all the time, every aisle. When they see me coming, they say, 'Okay, Manjit, what are you selling me today?' And I say, 'This—deodorant or candy bars—just try it, just try it. If you don't like it you bring it back. Just try it.' "

"Do your customers feel pressured?" I ask.

"Not at all. Not at all. They like me. My smile is my power. When I am back in India for three weeks to see my mother-in-law, I come back and people are asking me, 'Where were you? We miss you.' The people, they like me. My smile is my power."

And it is. After more probing on my part, I come to realize that, much to my and Dave Bernauer's disappointment, Manjit has no secret, no special sales technique that can be analyzed, systematized, and trained in across the entire Walgreens network. She simply has a uniquely winning personality and the drive to want to put it to use every day.

However, one thing did catch my attention: Manjit hasn't always been this successful at Walgreens. She has worked for them for more than three years but has only recently started to gain national attention for her performance.

"What happened?" I ask.

"Mr. K came. Mr. K is very friendly, very positive. It is a different place here now."

Mr. K, it turns out, is Jim Kawashima, Manjit's store manager. Jim is a diffident but articulate young man from San Diego who seems to make a habit of resuscitating troubled stores. Manjit's store is his third turnaround success story in the last four years.

Although he didn't hire her, according to Manjit, he has been the impetus for her leap to sustained excellence. He paid attention to some of her quirks and quickly figured out how to leverage these quirks into performance.

For example, Manjit loves numbers. One might almost say she is fixated on them. Back in India she was an athlete—a runner and, of all things, a weightlifter—and had always thrilled to the challenge of measured performance. Somehow Jim picked up on this and so now the back office walls are plastered with charts and figures, showing Manjit's sales performance as compared to her peers in the store, the district, and the entire Walgreens network. Manjit's scores, always at the top, are circled in red felt-tip pen.

Manjit is acutely aware of all this. In fact, on the day I interviewed her, one of the first things out of her mouth was, "On Saturday I sold three hundred forty-three low-carb candy bars. On Sunday three hundred sixty-seven. Yesterday one hundred ten and today one hundred five."

"Do you always know how well you're doing?" I ask.

"Yes. Every day I check Mr. K's charts. Even on my day off I make a point to come in and check my numbers."

Another characteristic of Manjit's is her love of public recognition. Most people like some kind of praise from their boss, but few show the intensity for it that Manjit does.

"I am famous around here," she tells me. "Managers everywhere say, 'Why can't you be like Manjit?' " She is joyful, buoyant.

Rather than chide her, as some managers would, to keep her ego in check so that others can take their turn in the spotlight, Jim nurtures this craving for attention and then channels it. Competing for space with the charts on the back office walls are dozens of photographs he has taken. All of them, with one exception, show Manjit, and whoever came in second that month, smiling proudly beside an aisle end-cap display. I ask Jim about the one exception.

"Is that one of the months she didn't win?"

"No." He grins. "She won that month as well, but in order to make the deadline for getting the photo into the Walgreens newsletter, I had to take the photo on her day off. Boy, did she let me have it! Mr. K, she said, if you need to take a picture on my day off, call me in. I will come right away."

Not all great managers share the same style as Jim Kawashima. Not even all great Walgreens managers share the same style as Jim. When I visited the manager who was given the privilege of opening Walgreens' four thousandth store, Michelle Miller, I found her back office wallpapered with work schedules, not charts, figures, and photographs. (I'll explain why in the next chapter.)

However, though they may not share his style, all great managers excel at doing with their people what Jim did with Manjit. They all excel at turning one person's talent into performance. This, in all its simplicity, is the role of great managers. In *First, Break All the Rules,* I used the analogy that great managers are catalysts, and this analogy still holds. At their best, great managers speed up the reaction between each employee's talents and the company's goals.

The chief responsibility of a great manager is not to enforce quality, or to ensure customer service, or to set standards, or to build high-performance teams. Each of these is a valuable outcome, and great managers may well use these outcomes to measure their success. But these outcomes are the end result, not the starting point. The starting point is each employee's talents. The challenge: to figure out the best way to transform these talents into performance. This is the job of the great manager.

One objection to this, of course, is that the manager is not the employee's agent; he is the company's agent. Although he may be interested in each employee's success, what happens when the goals of the employee and the goals of the company don't coincide? When push comes to shove, shouldn't the company's goals come first? Shouldn't the company's goals trump the employee's? The inherent conflict of the manager's role—should he serve the company or the employee?—is why I call this section "A View from the Middle".

Although this conflict has preoccupied business theorists and workplace lawmakers for decades, none of the great managers I've interviewed have much time for it. They seem confused whenever I bring it up, as though somewhere along the line I've missed the point. In their eyes, there is no conflict. Sure, they are aware that as managers they exist to serve the ends of the company, as all employees do. But they know instinctively that the only way for a manager to serve the company is to serve the employee first.

Here's their logic:

The manager's unique contribution is to make other people more productive. He may be charged with other responsibilities, such as selling or designing or leading, but, when it comes to the managing aspect of his job, he will succeed or fail based on his ability to make his employees more productive working with him than they would be working with someone else. And the only way to pull this off, they say, is to make your employees believe, genuinely believe, that their success is your primary goal.

Pause for a moment and recall the best manager you have ever worked for. What did she want from you? What did she want *for* you? What were most of your conversations about? Try to identify her main motives toward you and your achievements.

If this person was indeed a great manager, I bet that, over time, you became convinced that she was deeply preoccupied with the challenge of making you as successful as possible. Of course, on some level you knew that she was being paid to serve the company's agenda, but somehow this agenda receded into the background and was replaced by the feeling that you and your success were her primary focus.

Secure in this belief, you were prepared to give her your very best. When you could have quit for the day, you reached down for that extra hour of effort. When you could have joined a group of naysayers, you offered her your loyalty and support. When, during times of uncertainty, you could have jumped ship, you gave her the benefit of the doubt and stuck around.

None of this means that she was soft on you. In fact she was probably tougher on you than some of your more mediocre managers. She had confidence in your talents and so she pushed you hard, harder than you would have pushed yourself. She challenged you to set your standards higher and showed you how to reach these standards. She painted a vivid picture of excellence in your role and coached or cajoled you to embody this picture. She may even have disagreed with you when you sought a promotion and told you that, given her understanding of your talents, you would be crazy to take that job.

So she was tough, expectant, demanding, but through it all, you never doubted that your success was the North Star, the guiding light around which all decisions were made. Even though, rationally, you were aware that you were a means to an end, emotionally, she never made you feel this way.

This, then, is how great managers resolve the dilemma of being caught in the middle between the company and the employee. They know that they are paid by the company to make you want to give your all, but they also know that you will give your all only if you feel supported, challenged, understood, and stretched to be as successful as your talents will allow. As a result, great managers know they have no choice. To do their job, they *must* start with your feelings. They *must* convince you that, in their eyes, your success is paramount.

I have written this as though they arrive at this conclusion by deductive logic, but it doesn't really happen that way. In interviews, their commitment to each employee's success appears to be driven less by logic than by intuition and instinct. This is because one of the talents most characteristic of great managers is an ability to derive satisfaction from seeing tiny increments of growth in someone else. Psychologically speaking, they really don't have a choice. They can't help but focus on helping you succeed because, given the way their brains are wired, they are immediately intrigued by you, and by the challenge of figuring out how to arrange the world so that you can experience the greatest success possible. This talent is commonly known as the coaching instinct.

Jim Kawashima clearly has it; you should have seen the expression on his face when he talked about Manjit and her successes.

Michelle Miller has it; when I asked her what she enjoyed most about managing, her immediate response was "Helping other people grow." And this wasn't just some feel-good answer. She has found and developed more than a dozen future store managers, and her reputation for developing others is now so widespread that Walgreens deliberately funnels many candidates with high potential through her store—in fact, two former trainees interrupted our interview, calling her from their stores, one for practical guidance, one for emotional support.

Indeed, every great manager I've ever interviewed has it. No matter what the situation, their first response is always to think about the individual concerned and how things can be arranged to help that individual experience success.

If you possess this talent, you'll know what I'm talking about. You won't waste your time pondering how to resolve the conflict between the needs of the company and the needs of the employee. To you, this is theoretical mumbo-jumbo. Instead, you'll set to work getting to know each of your people and trying to figure out how, where, and when each of them can succeed. You'll find the time to watch each one's performance closely. You'll offer a suggestion here, a tip there, and then support them as they attempt to put your coaching into practice. Each little improvement you see, each new victory, no matter how small or ephemeral, will register with you and supply the fuel you need to keep coaching and guiding.

And should one or two of them show no signs of growth, you won't torture yourself about whether to confront them, as the company would like, or to let their mediocrity slide, as they might like. Of course you'll confront them. You know that if you let them languish in mediocrity, you'll be serving no one's interests, least of all theirs. So you'll tweak their role, or change it entirely, or perhaps even counsel them out of the company. You'll try anything you can think of that might lead to their success.

On the flip side, if you don't possess this coaching instinct, much of this will seem foreign to you. Yes, on a rational level you will probably appreciate the need for managers to help other people grow, but you won't be fascinated by this growth, and drawn to it, and thrilled by it the way great managers are. In fact, because your brain is not tuned to a frequency that picks up other people's small improvements, over time your manage-ment responsibilities will quickly seem like thankless chores.

This, at any rate, is what happened to me. I am not a natural coach. I am a focused person, a project person, a person who likes to work in series, from one completed assignment to the next. In short, I like getting things done. From my perspective, the annoying thing about people is that they are never done. They are always, and only, works in progress. And to me, this progress is frustratingly hard to detect.

It's not that I dislike people—I enjoy their company, their ideas, their achievements. It's just that I can't see them growing. When I was a manager, employees would come into my office to discuss some aspect of their work and ask for advice, which I would happily provide, and then they would walk out looking exactly the same as when they walked in. I couldn't see any dif-ference, any growth.

Of course, they *were* different. They *were* growing. Not right then, perhaps, but a couple of days later, after they had figured out how to incorporate my advice into their readiness and their style, they would be slightly better at explaining a point to a client, or writing up a report, or presenting a certain slide, or whatever it was that we had discussed. My problem was that I couldn't see these small, incremental improvements. They didn't register.

When I interviewed Michelle Miller, the Walgreens store manager, she was able to remember not only the names of all the store managers whom she had helped to develop, but also, when I probed, she could recall the particular challenges that each faced and how she helped each to rise to those challenges.

In contrast, when I received this recent e-mail from a former colleague

> Man, I miss you tons. Where are you in California? Maybe we can grab a drink when I am in your city. We can talk about the good old days . . . like when you taught me about Q12 in your hotel in Atlanta . . . remember that?

I realized that the answer was no, I didn't remember at all.

I have a contribution to make, but excellence in managing other people is not it. The irony is not lost on me that, after a lifetime of interviewing, I know more about great managing than I ever thought I would know, but I can't do it. In this sense, I'm a shining example of the maxim "If you can't do, teach. And if you really can't do, consult about it."

In fact, I'd wager that you are a better manager than I am, or will ever be. I don't lack the drive, or the relationships, or the conceptual ability to manage—I think I have all of these. It's just that, for whatever reason, the clash of my chromosomes perhaps, or my early childhood experiences, I am wired neither to see nor to derive satisfaction from seeing small increments of growth in other people. I see people as a means to a performance end. Great managers do not. No matter what the performance pressures placed upon them by their company, great managers see people as an end unto themselves.

As my mentor, Dr. Donald O. Clifton, used to say, the American Management Association has got it wrong. The AMA's slogan, "Getting work done through people", misstates the essence of great management. To capture this essence, they should change it to "Getting people done through work".

## A VIEW FROM THE TOP

*"What do great leaders actually do and what talents do you need to do it?"*

So, if great managers turn one person's talent into performance, what do great leaders do? What unique thing do they accomplish that makes them great leaders?

First, we need a good definition of leadership.

In *Alice Through the Looking Glass,* Humpty Dumpty famously pours scorn on word definitions. When Alice challenges him that the word "glory", which he has just defined as "a nice knock-down argument", doesn't actually mean "a nice knock-down argument", he replies, "When *I* use a word it means just what I choose it to mean—neither more nor less."

This is a quirky perspective, which Humpty Dumpty then plays out into a theory that you must be the master of your words before they master you. For our purposes, this position isn't much help. Getting the right definition of leadership is no academic exercise. If, as Warren Bennis says, at least 15 percent of an organization's success is due to leadership, we need to know how to identify people who have it, or at least the potential for it. We need to know how to create an environment that nurtures it and celebrates it. We need to know which aspects of it can be trained and which are innate. None of these is possible if each of us chooses to give "it" a different meaning.

A great many people have taken a crack at defining leadership. For example, in *Primal Leadership,* the authors detail nineteen traits that effective leaders are supposed to possess, traits such as "emotional self-control", "transparency", "initiative", and "building bonds", all of which, they tell us, are learnable. Rudy Giuliani, who undoubtedly knows a thing or two about leading, offers a tighter definition. In his book, titled simply *Leadership,* he narrows it down to six traits: know your values; be hopeful; be prepared; show courage; build great teams; and, above all, love people.

Even the United States Army has weighed in. They believe that seven is the required number of traits. According to their book *Be, Know, Do: Leadership the Army Way,* what you need to lead is a combination of loyalty, duty, respect, selfless service, honour, integrity, and personal courage, the first letters of which, happily, spell out LDRSHIP.

While most of these attempts to define leadership deserve to be taken seriously, perhaps, like Humpty Dumpty, you are dismissive of definitions. Perhaps you think that leadership is akin to art: you don't need to define it, because you'll know it when you see it.

All right then, in the paragraphs below I am going to describe a specific event. This was the kind of high-intensity situation that demands the very best of every participant and that transforms a select few into heroes. I am going to highlight three of these heroes: Randy Fogle, Joe Sbaffoni, and Dr. Kelvin Ke-Kang Wu. As you read, ask yourself whether what each of them did under extreme pressure meets your criteria for leadership. (My description of this event is drawn from two primary sources: Peter Boyer's account in *The New Yorker,* and the book *Our Story,* written by the survivors.)

On the evening of July 24, 2002, a crew of nine miners, supervised by crew boss Randy Fogle, was working the coal face of the Quecreek mine in Somerset, Pennsylvania. This particular face, called One Left, lay more than 240 feet below ground and could be reached only after navigating a tunnel a mile and a half long. This tunnel angled steadily down from the mine's entrance until about halfway in, when, owing to the contours of the coal seam, it dipped down for about six hundred feet before rising again in a slight upward slope that culminated at the One Left face.

In the Quecreek mine the actual digging was done by a continuous-mining machine. This is a sixty-ton piece of heavy equipment that stands at the face, gouges out chunks of coal, scoops them up, and then feeds them back on a conveyor belt to the waiting miners. The miner operating this machine usually stands to the right of it, using a remote control strapped to his hip, while the remainder of the crew hangs back and to the left of the machine.

Adjacent to the Quecreek mine was the old Saxman mine. Abandoned for decades, this mine had filled with water, creating the equivalent of a huge underground lake. A few hours into the shift on the 24th, the continuous-mining machine was digging into the coal seam as usual when it was suddenly hurled backward by the force of more than seventy million gallons of water pouring into the mine. The continuous-mining machine had broken through and pierced the lake.

After the initial panic and confusion, three things became clear to the miners. First, they were not going to be able to walk out of the mine. The water had rushed in at such a rapid rate— more than eighteen thousand gallons a minute—that, back toward the entrance of the mine, the six-hundred-foot dip in the tunnel had been overwhelmed by the flood, blocking their escape route.

Second, and counterintuitively, they saw that the safest place to huddle was back at the One Left coal face. Because the tunnel angled up from the dip, the coal face actually represented the highest available elevation in the mine. It would be the last place to be submerged as the mine filled with water.

Third, they realized that one of their number was missing. When the water burst through the coal face, the miner operating the mining machine, Mark "Moe" Popernack, standing to the right of the machine, jumped even farther to the right to avoid getting swept away. This undoubtedly saved his life at that moment, but it also cut him off from the rest of his crew, who all scrambled back and to the left as the water came down upon them. The wide torrent now created an impassable barrier for Moe, stranding him in a tiny space at the far right-hand edge of the coal face.

Although he was temporarily out of harm's way, his longer term prospects were not good. The two-hundred-foot-wide coal face was not horizontal, but angled steeply down from its high point on the far left to its lowest elevation on the extreme right. The water was pouring in through a hole about twenty feet in from the right-hand edge. Every miner except Moe had jumped to the left of the torrent. But Moe had jumped to the right, and now, stuck over on the lower side, he would inevitably be drowned many hours before the others.

Crew boss Randy Fogle didn't know how, or if, they were all going to get out of the mine, but he knew that he couldn't stomach the prospect of standing on the safe side of the torrent, watching one of his crew drown. Moe, he decided, had to be rescued. But how? At first he wondered if they could just wait for the water to slow down enough for Moe to wade across. After watching the water speed past them at more than ninety miles an hour, he realized that any slowing down wouldn't happen for hours, maybe days. They didn't have that kind of time.

Finally, he concluded that their only chance was to drive one of the front-end loaders right to the edge of the water, extend the scoop arm across, and have Moe jump into it. In the miners' words, "It was an outlandish idea. What if the water swept the scoop down the entry? After all, it had already pushed the sixty-ton miner twenty feet back. Whoever was driving the scoop would probably go down with it. And what if Moe missed the bucket when he jumped?"

No matter how outlandish an idea it was, Randy seized on it as their best shot. He climbed into the loader and started it up. "I felt it around a little bit, you know, and I got to a point I couldn't go much farther. I yelled at Moe, 'Far enough?' He shook his head no. I thought, Oh, boy, this is getting pretty touchy here. So I wiggled around a couple more feet and I yelled, 'You make it now?' "

Moe looked down at the water, steadied himself against the rock wall, and leaped "headfirst, with my hands out. I felt that hard steel and slid right into the back of the bucket and just stayed there until Randy got me across where they all were."

With Moe safe, Randy allowed himself a moment of calm. "We're all together now, we're all going to go as a team. We're all going to drown or we're all going to get out of this mess somehow." As the water level rose steadily, Randy maneuvered his crew into a small air-pocket at the left edge of the coal face and hunched down to wait.

Up on the surface, the rescue efforts were moving rapidly. The flood began a little after 9:00 p.m. on Wednesday night. By 3:15 a.m. the following morning, engineers had already guessed (correctly, as it turned out) what the miners' final position might be, had used a global positioning system device to pinpoint the surface equivalent of this position (a plowed field just off Route 985), and had set up a drill rig and begun to dig. They knew that nine miners were missing, and so their first priority was to dig a six-inch hole straight down into the mine so that some form of communication could be established with the survivors, if indeed there were any.

Among the growing throng of experts watching the drill's progress was Joe Sbaffoni, the bituminous division chief for Pennsylvania. Like everyone he was anxious for the drill to penetrate the mine as quickly as possible—only then would they know whether this operation was about life rescue or body recovery. And so, like everyone, he was thrilled when, at 5:00 a.m., the drill bit burst through the roof of the mine and somebody down there hit it with a hammer nine times, signaling that all nine had somehow survived the initial flood.

His celebration was short-lived. The original idea had been to lower a two-way microphone down the six-inch hole into the mine so that they could communicate in detail with the miners, but he soon saw that this was impossible. The moment the drill broke through the mine roof, a powerful geyser of air surged back up the hole and vented into the open air.

Immediately Joe knew what had happened. The drill had punctured the precious air pocket that was holding the waters at bay and keeping the miners alive. With the pocket deflating, the speed of the waters' rise would now increase. In a cruel and unforeseeable turn of events, the effort to establish contact with the survivors had only served to hasten their deaths.

Joe and his colleague John Urosek realized that the only hope for the miners was to pump new air down into the mine at high pressure, and at the same time stop up the geyser of air rushing out of the hole. This would create an artificial air pocket that would both supply the miners with breathable air and slow down the water's rise. Pumping new air into the mine proved quite straightforward—they ran a line down and turned on the air pump. But how could they stop the geyser?

The all-star team of engineers at the rescue site threw suggestions at one another, but all were rejected as being either ineffectual or too time-consuming. Finally Joe remembered that most fire departments had a store of inflatable airbags for use in delicate rescue situations. If they could squeeze some of these airbags down into the hole, arrange them around the drill machinery, and inflate them, then maybe the geyser would be plugged. He called the local fire department, secured the airbags, and feverishly shoved them down into the hole. "It was hard. The air was blowing 'em back up. But we got them air bags down there as best we could and blew 'em up as best we could."

Although the rescuers were unsure whether their efforts were having any measurable effect on the conditions in the mine, they clung to the artificial air bubble plan as their organizing principle. Over the next three days, as they struggled to overcome broken drill bits, impenetrable layers of rock, and unexplained silence from the miners below, they drew inspiration from the theory that so long as the air pumps kept pumping and the inflatable bags held fast, there was still some hope. The Sbaffoni Method, as the Pennsylvania governor labelled it, became their rallying cry.

One of the concerns gnawing at the rescuers was the pressure. Not the pressure of the situation, although this was intense, but the atmospheric pressure in the mine. As the rising waters pressed against the air pocket from below and the pumped-in air pressed against the water from above, the atmospheric pressure inside the air pocket increased. The miners themselves didn't feel significant discomfort from this, but with their empty water bottles crunching up as though squeezed by an unseen hand, they were certainly aware of it. They knew, as did the rescuers on the surface, that if they were pulled to the surface before the pressure in the air pocket had been lowered, then, like a scuba diver who ascends too quickly, they would suffer the bends.

Nine decompression chambers were being brought in by the navy to deal with this possibility, but another expert on hand, Dr. Kelvin Ke-Kang Wu, suggested a different solution. Dr. Wu was the chief of the federal mine agency's Mine Waste and Geotechnical Engineering Division. He agreed with the consensus opinion that the air pocket was the only thing keeping the miners alive, but rather than tie all his hopes to the Sbaffoni Method, he focused his attention on the water pumps. He reasoned that the only way to ensure a safe rescue of the miners was to equalize the atmospheric pressure between the air pocket and the surface. And, since it was the advancing water pressing on the air pocket that was causing the pressure to rise, the only way to equalize the pressure was to slow, and ultimately reverse, the water's rise.

Huge pumps had already been brought to the mine's entrance and were now hard at work draining more than thirty thousand gallons a minute from the mine. Dr. Wu calculated that only when the pumps had lowered the water level in the mine to 1,829 feet would the pressure be equalized and a safe rescue possible. He therefore advocated that the big drill, currently boring a thirty-inch hole down toward the miners through which each would be lifted to the surface, halt its drilling at 1,860 feet until they had confirmation that the water had fallen below the 1,829-foot level.

In hindsight it is obvious how sound Dr. Wu's calculations were, but in the overheated climate of the rescue effort, they seemed needlessly precise. When every instinct in every rescuer's body was to reach the trapped miners as quickly as possible, when on-site physicians were cautioning against the dangers of hypothermia from extended submersion in fifty-degree water, here was this Dr. Wu telling them to stop digging thirty-one feet short of their prize. They were dismissive, impatient. They wanted to press on.

In the face of this resistance, Dr. Wu remained calm, rational, and resolute. He would not move off his number, 1,829 feet—"Dr. Wu's magic number," as it came to be called.

Peter Boyer described what happened next. Having persuaded the assembled experts that he was right, "Dr. Wu excused himself, got in his car, and headed home for a shower, supper, and a few hours' sleep. He had just gone to bed when his telephone rang. It was a colleague, asking him to return to the command center. The big drill was making good progress, and people were beginning to agitate for pushing through to the mine as soon as possible. Dr. Wu dressed, and returned to Somerset, where a meeting was convened in the command centre just after midnight. . . Dr. Wu again made his case that it was too risky to breach the mine with another hole when the water was still up that high. Again he prevailed. The meeting concluded at about 1:30 a.m."

Two days later, his resolve was rewarded. When the big drill inched to within twenty feet of the miner's sanctuary, he had it halt and wait as he watched the water level slowly falling through 1,832 feet, 1,831, 1,830, until it reached the magic number, 1,829 feet. Only then did he release the drill for its final push into the air pocket. If his calculations were correct, the atmospheric pressure inside the air pocket would be normalized. They were. It was. The miners could now be safely hauled out and up to the surface.

After the rescue, having held his team together throughout their seventy-seven-hour ordeal, Randy Fogle had one last decision to make. His crew wanted to sign with a lawyer who was prepared to sue to hold someone accountable for the disaster. Someone, somewhere had been negligent and should be made to pay.

Despite the obvious financial incentives, Fogle broke ranks and refused to be a party to the lawsuit. Looking back, he could see nothing the company or the state could have done to prevent the flood. They were digging where they were supposed to dig. They knew the Saxman mine was close by, but according to the most reliable maps available, it was still about three hundred feet beyond the coal face. Yes, the ceilings of the mine were dripping with water, but many safe mines were so-called wet-mines. The wetness was by no means a sign that something terrible was about to happen. The mine had even been inspected by a state safety team a couple of weeks before the disaster.

His crew could seek damages if they wished. But, no, he would not. From his perspective no one was to blame. No one caused the disaster, except maybe Mother Nature. In Randy's words, "It's Mother Nature you're messing with, and it's you and her. That's one of the challenges. You're playing against a force that is awesome. You can never control it because it's bigger than you are. I mean she's wicked."

• • •

Each of these men—Randy, Joe, and Dr. Wu—performed in an extraordinary fashion, and each of them has rightly been recognized as a key figure in the successful rescue of all nine miners. But in reading of their exploits, what did you actually see?

You saw Randy Fogle take the initiative not only to devise the best way to save Moe, but also to jump into the loader himself and manoeuvre the arm over the raging waters.

You saw Joe Sbaffoni's MacGyver-like creativity. When the initial plan to communicate with the miners failed, he quickly improvised a new plan and even figured out which local materials could be used to execute it.

You saw Dr. Wu stick to his guns when everyone else was agitating for a precipitous push into the mine.

And finally, you saw Randy Fogle display the integrity to resist financial temptation.

But did you see leadership?

Most organizations certainly seem to think so. When organizations say that each and every employee can be a leader, more often than not they are referring to those four behaviours: initiative, creativity, the courage of one's convictions, and integrity. And, in one sense, they are right to call attention to these behaviours. Each employee *can* take initiative, and figure out new ways of getting things done, and show resolve, and take full responsibility for his actions. And, yes, if each employee does these things, the organization will be stronger for it.

But they err when they label these behaviours leadership. In my description of the Quecreek mining disaster, you saw examples of admirable men doing heroic things, but you didn't necessarily see leadership. I'm not saying that the three men I highlighted aren't leaders. In fact, as I'll reveal a little later in this chapter, one of them certainly is. I'm simply saying that the particular actions I chose to include in my description do not, in and of themselves, constitute leadership.

Randy Fogle showed integrity in refusing to join his crew's lawsuit. This doesn't make him a leader, though. It makes him a person of integrity. Yes, all leaders should possess integrity, but so should the rest of us. Integrity is not just a desirable leadership trait; it is a desirable human trait.

The same can be said of the other three behaviours. If you take initiative, improvise creative solutions to changing circumstances, and have the courage of your convictions, you will be a formidable and effective human being, and surely an asset to any organization, but you will not necessarily be a leader.

So what does define leadership? What do leaders get done that is distinct from what ordinary people of initiative, creativity, resolve, and integrity get done?

From all my research, this is the only satisfactory definition I've found:

**Great leaders rally people to a better future.**

And the two key words in this definition are "better future". What defines a leader is his preoccupation with the future. In his head he carries a vivid image of what the future could be, and this image drives him on. This image, rather than, say, goals of outperforming competitors, or being individually productive, or helping others achieve success, is what motivates the leader.

Don't misunderstand. An effective leader might also be competitive, achievement oriented, and a good coach. But these are not the characteristics that make him a leader. He is a leader if, and only if, he is able to rally others to the better future he sees. Two hundred and fifty years ago this fixation on the future sounded like this, from one of George Washington's circulars to the Congress:

> The Citizens of America, placed in the most enviable condition, as the sole lords and proprietors of a vast tract of continent . . . are now by the late satisfactory pacification, acknowledged to be possessed of absolute freedom and independency; They are, from this period, to be considered as actors on a most conspicuous theatre, which seems to be peculiarly designed by providence for the display of human greatness and felicity.

Fifty years ago it sounded like this, from Kennedy's debate with Nixon:

> Therefore I think the question before the American people is, are we doing as much as we can do? Are we as

strong as we should be? Are we as strong as we must be if we are going to maintain our independence, and if we are going to hold out the hand of friendship to those who look to us for assistance, to those who look to us for survival? I should make it very clear that I do not think we are doing enough, that I am not satisfied as an American with the progress we are making. This is a great country, but I think it could be a greater country; and this is a powerful country, but I think it could be a more powerful country. . . It's time America started moving again.

Today, it sounds like this, from Tony Blair's speech to his party conference in October 2003 (incidentally, the original conference title read "Fairness for All", Blair insisted it be changed to "A Future, Fair for All"):

The reason I bang the drum for change is I get so angry that it takes so long, restless at how much there is to do. I want us to go faster, further. . . Get rid of the false choice; principles or no principles. Replace it with the true choice: forward or back. I can go only one way. I've not got a reverse gear.

In quoting Tony Blair, my point is not that the future he sees is, in an objective sense, the "right" future—as I write, roughly half of Britons agree with him, while the other half disagree passionately. Nor is my point that effective leaders, by lacking a "reverse gear", refuse to backtrack and seek an alternative route when they realize they've made a mistake. On the contrary, only the ineffective leader clings consistently to his chosen route when all evidence suggests he has hit a dead end.

My point is simply that leaders are fascinated by the future. You are a leader if, and only if, you are restless for change, impatient for progress, and deeply dissatisfied with the status quo. Later in his debate with Nixon, Kennedy found himself repeating the same phrase over and over again:

> I am not satisfied when the United States had last year the lowest rate of economic growth of any industrialized society in the world . . .
>
> I am not satisfied when the Soviet Union is turning out twice as many scientists and engineers as we are . . .
>
> I am not satisfied when many of our teachers are inadequately paid . . .
>
> I am not satisfied when I see men like Jimmy Hoffa, in charge of the largest union in the United States, still free . . .
>
> I am not satisfied until every American enjoys his full constitutional rights . . .

"I am not satisfied." This is the mantra of the leader. As a leader you are never satisfied with the present, because in your head you can see a better future, and the friction between the "what is" and the "what could be" burns you, stirs you up, propels you forward. This is leadership.

Thus far my examples have all fallen within the political

sphere, but of course leaders—those who have a passionate belief in a better future—can be found in any sphere. The school superintendent who constantly pushes his teachers to come up with more effective ways to help children learn is a leader, as is the pastor who rallies his congregation with images of a more faithful community; the store manager who begins every staff meeting with a vivid description of the best customer stories from the previous day; and the sports coach who challenges his team to visualize what the perfect play would look like. Whenever a person strives to make others see a better future, there is leadership.

And what talents do you need to lead? If the core talent of great managers is an instinct to coach others toward success, then optimism and ego are the talents underpinning all great leadership.

The need for a talent for optimism is almost self-evident. As a leader you must believe, deeply, instinctively, that things can get better. You don't describe your images of the future because you want to put a brave face on things, or because you hope that you will be able to inspire other people. Others may become inspired, and you may recognize that as important, but you don't do it for this reason. You do it because you can't help it. You do it because you see the future so vividly, so distinctly that you can't get it out of your head. No matter how intense the present, the possibilities of the future seem to you even more intense. You have no choice but to do everything in your power to make them real.

The epitome of this kind of "I have no choice" optimism can be found in Winston Churchill's speech to Parliament in May

1940. Called in from the political wilderness to lead Britain out of crisis, Churchill was being pressured from all sides to sue Germany for peace. The fall of Poland, Belgium, the Netherlands, Denmark, and France convinced some that the German blitzkrieg was unstoppable. Since it was only a matter of time before Great Britain too succumbed to the Nazis, the most prudent course, they said, would be to seek peace terms whereby Britain wouldn't challenge German sovereignty in Europe so long as Germany promised not to invade the British Isles. If they were expecting a rational policy of appeasement, they were quickly disappointed. Churchill, the irrational optimist, had other ideas:

> You ask, What is our policy? I say it is to wage war by land, sea and air. . . . That is our policy.
>
> You ask, What is our aim? I can answer in one word. It is victory. Victory at all costs—victory in spite of all terrors, victory, however long and hard the road may be, for without victory there is no survival.
>
> I take up my task in buoyancy and hope. I feel sure that our cause will not be suffered to fail among men.

Appeasement may have been the rational policy, but Churchill just couldn't see it. All he could see was a future where the Nazis were defeated and Britain victorious. And so he had no choice. Victory became his aim and his policy. This optimistic vision of the future seized him, overrode all other considerations, and commanded him to act.

Here I don't mean to imply that all leaders are blessed with a perennially sunny disposition. Some leaders are, but others are decidedly grouchy, and a few, such as Abraham Lincoln and Churchill himself, even struggle with depression, Churchill's "black dog".

When I say leaders are optimistic I mean simply that nothing—not their mood, not the reasoned arguments of others, not the bleak conditions of the present—nothing can undermine their faith that things will get better.

Cast your mind back to crew boss Randy Fogle for a moment. I've described how he took the initiative to rescue Moe from the other side of the floodwaters and how he refused the temptation to join his crew in their lawsuit. And I've said that initiative and integrity do not, in and of themselves, constitute leadership. But I don't want to leave you with the impression that Randy isn't a leader.

What I didn't reveal was that, throughout their ordeal, he was the one who rallied the others to believe that they were going to be rescued. He was the one who bullied them to build a wall out of discarded cinderblocks in the hope, vain to some, that it might hold back the waters for one minute more. He was the one who draped a tarpaulin across the tunnel so that they would be spared the sight of the waters climbing up toward them. He was the one who answered their despair with detailed descriptions of all that the rescuers would be doing to free them from the mine. Here's one example, in Randy's own words:

I was hoping the water had flooded out into the mine

entrance so that they could start with the big pumps, just to get it taken care of. The guys asked me a lot of questions about it. They said, "Well, where are they going to get them big pumps at? They don't make pumps that big." I said, "It's unbelievable the pumps they make today." And they said, "Well, how are they going to get them here?" I said, "They'll fly them. Whatever it takes, they're going to get them here. They'll be here, don't worry."

This little speech might not be as eloquent as Churchill's, but so what? This is not mere initiative. Nor is it simple integrity. This, in all its optimistic glory, is leadership. Randy knew how dire their predicament was, but somehow he was able to summon the spirit and the optimism to rally his people to see, and to act as though they could see, a better future. Build a wall to slow the rising tide. Pull the tarpaulin over so that we can keep the water out of sight and out of mind. Believe that the rescuers are moving hell itself to stem these high waters. Believe, like I do, that we are going to get out of here alive. Believe.

These are the encouragements of a leader.

If you don't feel this way, if you are, by nature, a little jaded, disillusioned by the motives of man and the capriciousness of fate, take heart. First, you will be right more often than the optimist. After all, there are many more ways that things can go wrong than right. And, second, there are jobs for you, jobs in which an innate scepticism can serve as a distinct advantage— in the legal department, for example, or strategic planning. (I'm joking. A little.) But, whatever you do, don't lead. Properly defined, the opposite of a leader isn't a follower. The opposite of a leader is a pessimist.

This doesn't mean that the best leaders are wide-eyed dreamers, delusional about or dismissive of present realities. On the contrary, the best leaders are markedly clear-eyed when it comes to assessing the challenges of the present. It simply means that, despite their realistic assessment of present challenges, they nonetheless believe that they have what it takes to overcome these challenges and forge ahead.

Which, inevitably, raises the whole question of ego.

The need for a leader to have a strong ego is rather less self-evident. Much has been written lately about the need for leaders to be humble, to downplay their egos, and, indeed, a review of the business pages reveals a motley crew of executives all of whom appear to have succumbed to a surfeit of ego. Bernie Ebbers at WorldCom; the Rigas family at Adelphia; Gary Winnick at Global Crossing; Ken Lay at Enron; Martha Stewart at Martha Stewart Omnimedia. The list is depressingly long, and growing.

However, no matter how reprehensible their actions may have been, to explain their misfortune as a function of excess ego is actually a misdiagnosis. The reputations of these executives fell not because their egos were too strong but because their principles were not strong enough. They had too little integrity, not too much ego.

The key thing about leading is not only that you envision a better future, but also that you believe, in every fibre of your being, that you are the one to make this future come true. You are the one to assume the responsibility for transforming the present into something better. From all my interviews with effective leaders I cannot think of one example in which the person lacked this craving to be at the helm, charting the course ahead. In fact, looking back through history, one can see that even seemingly saintly leaders possessed this need to stake outstanding claims, this preternatural self-belief.

Think of Mahatma Gandhi setting out from his home to make the 150-mile trek to the coastal town of Dandi in order to extract salt from the sea, in symbolic defiance of the British salt tax. You and I might have worried that no one would notice us, and that we would wind up at the beach all by ourselves, lamely boiling our saucepan of seawater. Gandhi didn't. He was confident that by the time he arrived tens of thousands would have joined him. And, of course, he was right.

Or think about Saint Paul returning to Jerusalem and informing the apostles that he, not they, knew what Jesus would have wanted for the young church, and that *they* should modify their practices to accord with *his* teachings, rather than the other way around. What gall. What ego.

Is "independent" a better descriptor than "ego"? Maybe. How about "self-assured"? Perhaps. "Self-confident"? Possibly. But "humble"? This seems a particularly odd word choice. Leaders don't set humble goals. They don't have humble dreams. They are not humble in their assessment of their own abilities. Virtually nothing about them is humble.

This doesn't mean that they think they have all the answers. On the contrary, the best leaders have a strong expertise orientation. They are curious and inquisitive, always on the lookout for the small insight, the novel perspective that might nudge them over the tipping point and give them an edge over their competition.

Nor does it mean that they are brash or abrasive. Some may be, but as Jim Collins has correctly pointed out, many of the most effective leaders are quite reserved.

Nor does it mean they are egomaniacal. The difference between a leader with a powerful ego and an egomaniac is how the ego is channeled. The effective leader takes his self-belief, his self-assurance, his self-confidence, and presses them into the service of an enterprise bigger than himself. For the egomaniac, the self is the enterprise.

But this does mean that they make outstanding claims to excellence. It does mean that their self-worth is inextricably wrapped up in both their appetite to make such claims and in their ability to realize them.

So if you want to help develop a budding leader, don't tell him to deflate his ego into humility, to lessen his dreams, to downplay his belief in himself. This is confusing, negating advice. Instead, challenge him to be more inquisitive, more curious, and thereby more vivid in describing his image of a better future, and then encourage him to channel his cravings and his claims toward making this image come true.

The necessity for leaders to possess optimism and ego serves to answer the age-old question: Are leaders born or are they made? They are born. A leader is born with an optimistic disposition or she is not. If she is not, then no amount of "optimism training" is going to make her view the world in an overwhelmingly positive, opportunistic light. Through repeated counselling and coaching, you might be able to make a person less pessimistic than she was before, but "less pessimistic" is not synonymous with "optimistic", any more than "less rude" is synonymous with "charming". To lead effectively, you must be unfailingly, unrealistically, even irrationally optimistic. Like it or not, this is not learnable.

The same applies to ego. Through careful nurturing you can make a person feel more self-confident and more self-assured than he used to be, but nothing you can do will ever imbue him with the kind of powerful, claiming ego that so characterizes the best leaders. He either has it or he doesn't. And, as a colleague of mine used to say, if he doesn't you can't give him mouth-to-ego resuscitation.

None of this implies that a person cannot be helped to improve as a leader. Of course she can. She can be helped to refine her picture of the future, even to change it entirely, and to employ ever more effective ways to present this future to her followers. But what you cannot help her do is see a better future, believe in this future, and have faith that she is the one to create it. Here, she's on her own.

· · ·

From all this, you can see the vital distinction between the role of the manager and that of the leader. Each is critically important to the sustained success of the organization, but the focus of each is entirely different.

The manager's starting point is the individual employee. He looks at her palette of talents, skills, knowledge, experience, and goals, and then uses these to design a specific future in which the individual can be successful. That person's success is his focus.

The leader sees things differently. He starts with his image of the future. This better future is what he talks about, thinks about, ruminates on, designs and refines. Only with this image clear in his mind does he turn his attention to persuading other people that they can be successful in the future he envisions. But, through it all, the future remains his focus.

You can play both roles, of course, but if you do, you must know when to change gears. When you want to manage, begin with the person. When you want to lead, begin with the picture of where you are headed.

Exactly how you can play each of these roles most effectively is the subject of the next two chapters. Here we will discuss the skills you can learn and refine as you strive to make the best use of your natural talents for managing and leading.

CHAPTER $3$

# The One Thing
# You Need to Know:
# Great Managing

## THE BASICS OF GOOD MANAGING

*"What skills will prevent you from failing
as a manager?"*

To grasp the One Thing you need to know about great managing does not mean ignoring the basics. Let's begin, then, with the four skills you simply must learn if you are not to fail as a manager.

First, you must select good people. The old maxim says, "You marry as is. You get any change if you're lucky." The same is undoubtedly true of hiring. Obviously, this doesn't mean that you can't help a person to learn and grow. It simply means that when you hire someone, you are hiring a human being blessed with certain predictable patterns of emotion, learning, memory, and behaviour. If these patterns are not to your liking, you are going to have to expend tremendous effort to eradicate them and forge entirely new ones. Since this effort would be more usefully deployed elsewhere, it will serve you well to take extreme care when inviting a new person onto your team.

Some managers claim that they don't have the time to select just the right person for the team. I have openings now, they say, and these openings must be filled. Good managers know the folly of this approach. They know that, when it comes to building the right team, time is a non-negotiable. You will spend the time. The only question is where you will spend it: on the front end, carefully selecting the right person, or on the back end, desperately trying to transform the person into who you wished he was in the first place.

When good managers say, in effect, "I love you just the way you are," they mean it. When average managers say it, they mean "I love you just the way you are going to be when I am finished with you." If you want to start on solid ground as a manager, you will avoid this wishful thinking and instead spend the time necessary to select a person who already possesses the talents you desire.

How can you do this? Well, since human beings are frustratingly complex, there are no silver bullets, but there are guidelines.

Know what talents you are looking for. Do you want someone who is competitive, or altruistic, or focused, or entrepreneurial, or creative, or analytical?

Ask open-ended questions and have clearly in mind what you are listening for. When I asked Michelle Miller what she enjoyed most about managing, I knew I was listening for some version of "helping other people grow and develop."

When you ask your open-ended questions, pay particular attention to the person's spontaneous response. Michelle's immediate response to my open-ended question was "I love helping other people succeed." This was significant. She didn't know what I was listening for, and there were many other plausible and socially acceptable answers, such as "I enjoy designing innovative solutions" or "I enjoy building high-performance teams" or "I enjoy problem solving," and each of these, admirable as they are, would have told me something about her. But she didn't land on any of these. Unaided, she landed on "helping other people succeed." This was her spontaneous answer, and so this was the answer I should use to predict her future behaviour.

Listen for specifics. The conventional wisdom holds that the best predictor of future behaviour is past behaviour. But this is incomplete. The best predictor of future behaviour is *frequent* past behaviour. In order to identify frequent past behaviour, you need to listen for specific examples of where and when the person has actually done what you are asking him about. For example, if you want to know if he is organized, ask him how he has structured his life so that he can be more efficient. If he can tell you a specific instance of when he did this, give him credit. However, if he describes in glorious but generic terms how very important it is to be organized, don't probe, don't ask him for more detail (every question you ask will reveal to him that he has not given you the answer you were looking for), simply chalk it up to the fact that organizing for greater efficiency is not a regular part of his daily life. If it were, it would be happening all the time, and thus, no matter when you asked him the question, he would have been able to pull from his recent memory a specific example.

The second basic skill of good management is this: Define clear expectations.

Since I have never met a confused productive employee, and neither, I imagine, have you, I probably don't need to belabour the need for clear expectations. All of us realize that confusion retards everything, from efficiency and focus (how can you distinguish a shortcut from a distraction if you don't know what the goal is?) to teamwork and partnership (how can you value the contributions of others if you don't know what your own contribution is supposed to be?) all the way to pride and satisfaction (if you don't know how your success is being measured, how will you ever get to feel successful?).

Despite this consensus need for clarity, however, it turns out that most managers are not very good at providing it. Research reveals that less than 50 percent of employees claim that they know what is expected of them at work. Apparently, while all managers know that setting clear expectations is paramount, most struggle to execute.

Some might blame this epidemic of confusion on the fast pace of change in the world today, but they would be mistaken. I have worked with teams in the high-tech field, where a product's half-life is measured in months but where every single employee could nonetheless strongly agree that they knew what was expected of them at work. And I have seen teams involved in more predictable work, such as front-desk clerks and delivery-truck drivers, where nobody was certain. I have even come across two teams involved in exactly the same kind of work, toiling away right next door to each other in the same building, separated only by the fact that, in one team, more than 90 percent of employees knew what was expected of them, whereas, in the other, only 15 percent did.

Confronted with this kind of local variation, the only possible conclusion is that the manager makes the difference. Either the manager brings clarity to her team or she doesn't.

How do good managers do this? How do they filter the many pressures and priorities passed down to them from above and distill from these a clear short-term focus and a clear set of metrics? One word can sum it up. They do it "constantly". They don't set goals once or twice a year, as their organization's policies may require them to. Instead they meet with each of their people a minimum of four or five times a year to check progress, offer advice, and agree on course corrections.

They begin at the point of hire, often with a powerful question such as "What do you think you get paid to do?" and then they continue to clarify expectations in virtually every meeting, every conversation, every presentation. Every time they talk with one of their people they see it as an opportunity to make expectations just that little bit clearer. This can be done tactfully, adjusting the tone to suit the individual, so as not to imply distrust or disappointment.

The third basic skill deals with praise and recognition. In his book *Bringing Out the Best in People,* Aubrey C. Daniels details the theory that every behaviour has a consequence, and that the consequence that follows a certain behaviour will significantly affect whether or not a person will repeat this behaviour. Consequences, he says, come in a variety of forms: positive/negative, future/immediate, certain/uncertain. Of these possibilities, the least powerful consequence is one that is uncertain, in the future, and negative. The most powerful is the opposite, one that is certain, immediate, and positive. Among other things, this helps explain why it can be so difficult to persuade someone to change to a healthier diet. After all, the consequences of not changing—namely that you might, in a few years time, become seriously overweight and that this obesity might, decades from now, prove fatal—are not nearly as persuasive as the certain and immediately wonderful taste of a doughnut.

Armed with this theory, Daniels reminds us that to bring out the best in our people we must carefully manage the consequences of their behaviours. If we want to see specific behaviours repeated, we must make sure that these behaviours meet with consequences that are certain, immediate, and positive. In short, we must come to be known as a manager who will recognize excellence immediately and praise it.

Unfortunately, obvious though this sounds, most of us do indeed need reminding. Research from such diverse organizations as Gallup, the American Management Association, and Towers Perrin reveals that less than a third of people report that they frequently receive praise or recognition for good work. This suggests either that they did something at a level of excellence and no one praised them for it, or that they haven't performed at a level of excellence recently. Of course, neither is a good thing.

Good managers, in contrast, don't need reminding of the power of praise. They seem to know instinctively that praise isn't merely a reaction to a great performance; it is a cause of it. In essence, they realize that the audience creates the performance. And since praise is a creative act, good managers say you should never worry about overpraising someone. So long as the performance warrants it, you can never praise someone too much, short of seeming insincere. Excellence is rarely a function of one-off achievement, but rather is a result of repeated practise and incremental improvement. Your job as a manager is to notice these incremental improvements and celebrate them. If you do, the person will be more likely to repeat them and so continue her virtuous climb toward excellence.

Conversely, if you withhold praise for good behaviours in the misguided belief that otherwise the employee will become complacent, then over time you will begin to see fewer and fewer of these behaviours. Having behaved in a certain way and been ignored for it, the employee will start to change his behaviour in order to get some kind of reaction from you—if not good, then bad will do, anything to avoid your seeming indifference. In fact, if your stars start to act up, it's a sure sign that you have begun to ignore the very behaviours that made them stars in the first place.

So, if you want to stimulate excellent performances from your people, make immediate praise a constant, predictable, and certain part of your management style.

The final skill of good management is disconcertingly warm and fuzzy: You must show care for your people. I would like to be able to replace this skill with one that is more hard-edged, more tangible, but there's no getting around the data. A multitude of research studies confirm that employees are more productive when they feel that someone at work cares about them. Actually the research confirms more than the causal link between caring and productivity. It also reveals that employees who feel cared about are less likely to miss workdays, less likely to have accidents on the job, less likely to steal, less likely to leave, and more likely to advocate the company to friends and family. No matter how you choose to measure performance, being cared about seems to drive it.

Human beings are herd animals; bonding is what we do. Put us in close proximity with other people and we will instinctively look for areas of common ground, areas where we can connect. In fact, so strong is our need to bond that, according to research into happy marriages, for those of us who met our spouse at university, the strongest predictor of whom we would marry was not that we shared the same subject, the same faith, the same nationality, or the same socioeconomic status, but rather that we were in the same halls. Apparently our appetite for bonding is so powerful that, if you force us to live in close quarters, a bunch of us are likely to marry one another.

So, bonding is in our blood. And when we have bonded, all kinds of other good things can happen. We can start to feel more secure, more willing to share our confidences, more willing to take risks, and more willing to support one another. As the manager, if you want these good things to happen, you must set the example and forge bonds of your own. Be deliberate about it. Be explicit. Tell your people that you care about them. Tell them that you want them to succeed. Keep their confidences. Learn about their personal lives, and, as far as you are able, be willing to accommodate the challenges of their personal lives into their work schedules.

None of this implies that good managers are soft on their people. On the contrary, good managers are willing to deal quickly with poorly performing employees precisely because they want each employee to succeed, and, on a visceral level, they cannot stand the sight of someone they care about staggering along at a mediocre level of performance. Counterintuitive though it may sound, the caring manager confronts poor performance early.

So, to manage effectively, you must genuinely care about the well-being and the success of each of your people. If you don't—if you find you resonate more with the predictability of projects than with the shifting emotional needs of people—then don't fake it. Fake caring is worse than no caring. Just do as I did and get out of management.

Pick good people, set clear expectations, recognize excellence and praise it, and show care for your people: these are the four basic skills of good managing. Do each of these well and you will be unlikely to fail as a manager. However, do each of these well and you will not be guaranteed success. Success as a manager will require of you an entirely different skill.

## GREAT MANAGERS PLAY CHESS

> *"What is the One Thing you need to know about great managing?"*

Quick, what's the key difference between checkers and chess?

Don't read on. Just think about it for moment. What's the key difference?

When I ask this question in seminars the two most common answers are "Chess is more difficult" and "Chess is more strategic." Both answers are true, of course, but both are unsatisfactory.

They leave the essence of the difference unexplained. Why exactly is chess more difficult, more strategic?

If you have a natural talent for managing (and have some familiarity with the game of chess), I'll bet you immediately landed on the right answer. The key difference between checkers and chess is that in checkers the pieces all move in the same way, whereas in chess all the pieces move differently. Thus, if you want to excel at the game of chess you have to learn how each piece moves and then incorporate these unique moves into your overall plan of attack.

The same is true for the game of managing. Mediocre managers play checkers with their people. They assume (or hope) that their employees will be motivated by the same things, driven by the same goals, desire the same kind of relationships, and learn in roughly the same way.

They probably wouldn't say it as baldly as I have just done, but their approach to managing gives it away. When they set expectations for their people, they define, in great detail, the exact behaviours they expect to see. When they coach their people, they identify which of these behaviours each employee is struggling with, and then tell the employee to work on these behaviours and practise them until they become habit. When they praise their people, they are most impressed by employees who have worked diligently to replace their natural style with these preset behaviours. In short, they believe that the job of the manager is to mold, or transform, each employee into the perfect version of the role.

Great managers don't. They do the opposite. The One Thing all great managers know about great managing is this:

**Discover What Is Unique About Each Person
and Capitalize on It.**

They know that even if employees are selected against the same set of talents or competencies, such is the complexity of human nature that the differences among these employees will far outweigh the similarities. And here I'm not referring to differences of race or nationality or sex or creed. These differences exist, of course, but when it comes to helping employees perform, they are almost irrelevant. If you accommodate these differences you will net some goodwill, but you won't necessarily net any increase in performance.

The differences I'm referring to are differences of personality. Your employees will differ in terms of how they think, how they build relationships, how they learn, how altruistic they are, how patient, how much of an expert they need to be, how prepared they need to feel, what drives them, what challenges them, and what their goals are. These differences of trait and talent are like blood types. They cut across the superficial differences of race and sex and capture the essential uniqueness of each individual.

The grand majority of these differences are enduring and resistant to change. So, given that your most precious resource as a manager is time, by far the most effective way to invest your time is to identify exactly how each employee is different and then, as in chess, figure out how you can best incorporate these differences into your overall plan of action.

The more one listens to the testimony of great managers, the clearer it becomes: great managing is not about transformation—if you dedicate yourself to transforming each employee into some predetermined perfect version of the role, you will wind up frustrating yourself and annoying the employee. Great managing is about *release*. It is about constantly tweaking the world so that the unique contribution, the unique needs, the unique style of each employee can be given free rein.

Your success as a manager will depend almost entirely on your skill at doing this. To grasp the full scope of this skill, consider what it looks like in the world of Walgreens, and more specifically in the world of Walgreens store 5881, in Redondo Beach, California, Michelle Miller's world. Michelle Miller, as you'll recall from the previous chapter, was the manager who was given the honour of opening Walgreens' four thousandth store. I am highlighting her not simply because she is patently so good at her job, but also because she has succeeded in capitalizing on the uniqueness of each employee, despite working for a huge corporation, one that, given its size, might be forgiven for insisting that each employee should be molded to squeeze into a carefully defined role. The fact that she is allowed to capitalize on each employee's uniqueness is a testament to Walgreens' wisdom. The fact that she does it so well is a testament to Michelle's.

## A WALK THROUGH A WALGREENS

*"How does one truly great manager do it?"*

If you want to feel, in vivid detail, the many pressures piled on managers today, walk a store with a store manager. It doesn't really matter which store you choose—it could be a Marks and Spencer, a WHSmith, a Boots, or your local supermarket—but spend any time with the store manager and you'll soon realize, if you don't already, just how many roles a modern manager is asked to play. Marketing, operations, sales, inventory control, human resources, information technology, it's all in the job description.

We'd been talking theory in Michelle's back office, but now it was time to see how things worked in the real world.

"Let's walk the store," I suggest. "I want to see it through your eyes."

So we walk into the aisles and immediately she changes. In the office she was relaxed, casual, all smiles and laughter, but out in the store she's a different person, intense, watchful, masterful Super Store Manager, minus the cape.

"See this? Here?" She is pointing to what seems to me like a perfectly decent display of Gatorade on sale for $1.69 per bottle. "This is wrong. A wasted opportunity. We should be advertising it at three dollars for two. No one buys just one bottle of Gatorade, so let's present it to the customers the way they want to buy it. Besides, I know we'll still make money at the three dollars for two bottles price point."

We walk on.

"Look. See here? All the toilet rolls are perfectly in line with the front of the shelf, with all their labels turned toward the customer. 'Facing' we call it. These toilet rolls are perfectly faced. That's Jeffrey. I know he worked this aisle last night."

We round a corner and see a couple of unsightly boxes in the middle of the aisle.

"Darn," she says under her breath. Then, louder, "Genoa! Genoa! Can we get these moved back into the stockroom? Right away please. Thank you!"

Her eyes land on another end cap.

"You see these?" She is pointing to an attractive display of hair-removal kits, one for women, called Finishing Touch, the other with the more manly moniker Micro-touch. "I'm gonna have to find a better place for these. I know from our computer system that these are selling well in other Walgreens stores, but for some reason they're not selling well in mine. We've got to move them somewhere else. Not sure where, right now. I'll have to think about it."

We turn into the last aisle.

"This whole aisle is going to have to be reset this week. Summer is around the corner, and when summer comes, people go outside, and when people run around outside, they tend to have accidents. So this is going to be our first-aid aisle. Band Aids. Bandages. Antiseptic creams. If you were to come back next week, this aisle would be piled high with them."

I ask her how she keeps all of these variables in her head at one time.

"That's what store management is," she replies blithely. "You have to have an eye for it. You have to have an eye for your store, an eye for your customers, an eye for your merchandise, and, of course, an eye for your people. It's all in the details. If you can't see them, if you come into your store every day with tunnel vision, then you're never gonna be successful, you know?"

I ask her which, of all of these many details, is most important to her, which task gets most of her attention.

"Scheduling," she replies.

"Really?" It wasn't the answer I was expecting.

"Yes. It doesn't matter what else I do, if I schedule the wrong employees together, then everything will fall apart. I've got to get everyone synced together, in harmony, complementary. 'Finding each person's forte' is what I call it. When I get that right, the rest takes care of itself."

Since, to my unpractised eye, her store seems like an exceptionally regimented workplace, I ask her for an example. How, exactly, does she schedule around each person's forte?

So she tells me how she capitalized on the rather unique contributions of two employees, first Jeffrey, and then Genoa.

She almost didn't hire Jeffrey. He is a Goth rocker, with hair dyed black, one side shaved, the other left long to cover his face. White shirt. Thin black tie. And a little nervous. During the interview he wouldn't meet her gaze, but kept looking away, eyes darting, nervous.

"But he wanted to go on the night shift, so I was like, hey, you know, maybe this guy can do the job. And then, after a couple of months of working with him I noticed something kinda cool. If I gave him a vague assignment such as 'Go up and down every aisle and straighten the merchandise,' it would take him all night to do it, when really it should have been just a two-hour pass. And even when it was done, it wouldn't be done well. But if I told him something very specific, such as "Put up all the risers for Christmas," he would do it perfectly, efficiently, and come back all pumped up, asking for more. Now, installing the Christmas risers is a big, complicated assignment. You've got to get the risers all symmetrical, with the right merchandise on each one, perfectly tagged, signed, and faced. But he would just do an awesome job and get it all done in a day."

Give Jeffrey a generic task and he would struggle. But give him a specific task, one that forces him to be accurate and analytical, and he excels. This, concluded Michelle, was Jeffrey's forte. This was where he would make the greatest contribution to the store. So, as all good managers do, she told him what she had deduced about him and praised him for it.

And a good manager would have left it at that. But Michelle, like all truly great managers, is a multiplier. She is not content merely to appreciate each person for his uniqueness, but rather is always searching for ways to capitalize on it. So, in thinking through the various responsibilities within the store, she devised a scheme to reassign these responsibilities in order to make Jeffrey's forte more valuable for the entire store.

In every Walgreens store there is a responsibility called "resets and revisions". "Resets" refers to the need to stock an entire aisle with new merchandise. These resets occur about once a month and usually coincide with a predictable change in customers' buying patterns. For example, toward the end of summer, a directive will come down from Walgreens HQ stating that the aisle of sun creams, after-sun creams, and lip balms should be restocked with allergy medicines since, as every sufferer knows, allergies return with the autumn. This is a reset.

A revision is a less extensive version of the same. Replace these toothpastes with this new and improved version. Display this new line of shorts on this end cap. Group all the low-carb candy bars together in the same section of the aisle. Revisions, although less time-consuming, occur much more frequently. Each aisle will require some form of revision at least once a week.

The usual arrangement in a Walgreens store is that each employee "owns" one aisle. In their aisle, they are responsible not only for serving customers, but also for facing the merchandise, keeping the aisle clean and orderly, tagging the merchandise with a Telxon gun, and all resets and revisions. Clearly, there are some benefits to this arrangement. It is simple, efficient, and allows each employee to feel a sense of personal responsibility for her section of the store. However, while not denying these benefits, Michelle decided that there was an even more efficient way of configuring the world to make the most of Jeffrey's forte.

Since he so loved the challenge of specific projects, she would change his job so that the only thing he had was specific projects, which, in the world of Walgreens, meant resets and revisions. He would be responsible for all resets and all revisions in every single aisle. This is a significant undertaking—one week's worth of revisions requires a binder three inches thick to detail them all—and so Jeffrey would have to devote his entire quota of hours to getting it all done. But, for three reasons, Michelle decided this dramatic reconfiguration of roles was worth the risk. First, Jeffrey, excited by the inherent challenge, would become more engaged. Second, the repeated practise would lead him to get better and better at it. And third, with Jeffrey bearing the entire load of resets and revisions, the other employees would be freed up to devote themselves to greeting and serving the customers. In her mind, it would be a quintuple win. Jeffrey would win, her other employees would win, so would the customers, so would she, and as a result, so would Walgreens.

And the store's performance proved her right. After her reorganization she saw not only increases in sales and profit, but also in that most critical performance metric, customer satisfaction—in the subsequent four months, her store netted 100 percent scores on Walgreens' mystery shopper programme.

So far, so very good. But, sadly, it didn't last. This perfect arrangement, this focused fit of forte to role depended on Jeffrey remaining content in his prescribed role. Annoyingly, he didn't remain content. Having experienced success as the reset and revision king his self-confidence grew and, after six months or so, he came to believe that he had more to offer store 5881. He wanted to move into management.

Confronted with these aspirations, Michelle was neither sad nor annoyed. She was intrigued. She watched Jeffrey's progress closely and decided that he might, if carefully positioned and coached, be able to do well as a manager. He would always be an analytical manager, careful and thoughtful rather than emotive, but in her view, there was room for this kind of manager in the wide world of Walgreens.

So she moved him into an assistant manager role, and in so doing, she utterly destroyed her carefully constructed configuration of roles and responsibilities. With Jeffrey promoted, who would take on the reset and revision role? Did she have anyone who shared Jeffrey's analytical talents and love of specific assignments? No, she didn't. So, what was her next move? Should she actively seek to hire someone who could play Jeffrey's old role, or should she simply revert back to the standard arrangement and reassign all resets and revisions to the employees in each aisle?

Michelle wasn't surprised by these questions. She didn't wake up one morning and say, Oh darn, I've got a problem here. Like all good chess players, she had been thinking a couple of moves ahead, and so when Jeffrey came to her with his desire to move up, she was ready.

Over in the cosmetics aisle worked an employee named Genoa, whom I mentioned earlier. Michelle had high hopes for Genoa. In her estimation, Genoa was a double threat. Not only was she adept at putting customers at ease—she remembered their names, asked good questions, was welcoming yet professional when answering the phone—but she was also a neat freak. Her cosmetics department was always perfectly faced, every product aligned, everything arranged just so. The overall impression was, for want of a better word, sexy. Her aisle made you want to reach out and touch the merchandise.

But there was a problem. Michelle wanted Genoa to apply her talents throughout the store, but she knew that Genoa and her direct supervisor, Kimberly, had a personality clash. Left to their own devices, these two were starting to grate on each other, wasting energy with their daily skirmishes. So Michelle decided to intervene.

"With this personality conflict, I know Kimberly isn't the best person to be training Genoa. I need to get Genoa out of the department and I need to train her on something so she feels some gratification in what she is doing, 'cause I need her to be a senior beauty advisor in a couple of months when Kimberly gets promoted to assistant manager."

Let's just pause for moment. Did you get all that? In this example, Michelle's got two employees who need to grow, three if you include Jeffrey, two of whom don't get along with each other, each with their own complement of talents and needs, a multitude of different roles to perform, and all of this growth, development, and performance has got to be worked out in full view of a constant flow of fickle, demanding customers.

If you have real talent for managing, you will be familiar with, even thrilled by, this dynamic complexity. But, if you don't . . . well, it's no wonder some people are overwhelmed by the challenges of management.

Michelle's solution was as elegant as it was simple. She decided to move Genoa out from under Kimberly and create for her a one-off role that would capitalize on her twin talents. To carve out this role she split Jeffrey's reset and revision role in two. She gave the revision part of it to Genoa so that the whole store could now benefit from her peculiar ability to arrange merchandise so attractively. But she didn't want the store to miss out on Genoa's gift for customer service, so she told her to focus on the revision role only between 8:30 a.m. and 11:30 a.m., and after that, when the store began to fill with customers on their lunch breaks, Genoa should change her focus back to them.

The reset role would stay with Jeffrey. Assistant managers don't usually have an ongoing responsibility within the store, but, Michelle reasoned, he was now so good at tearing an aisle apart and rebuilding it again that he could easily finish a major reset during one five-hour stint.

And just like that Michelle pulled off another quintuple win. Genoa was given a chance to extend her range. Michelle was spared having to deal with the constant clashes between Genoa and Kimberly. Jeffrey was allowed to keep strutting his reset stuff. The customers benefited from a more attractive, more organized store. And so, once again, Walgreens netted excellent results from store 5881.

By the time you read this, it's likely the Genoa-Jeffrey configuration has outlived its usefulness and Michelle has moved on to design other equally effective configurations. This ability to keep tweaking the world so as to capitalize on the uniqueness of each employee is, in all its intricate, ever-changing glory, the essence of great management.

## GREAT MANAGERS ARE ROMANTICS

*"What are the benefits of individualization?"*

This heading doesn't mean what you might think, but it should become clear shortly.

At present, I'm concerned that I've left you with the impression that Michelle's creative choreographing of roles and responsibilities was her attempt to make the best of a bad job; that if she had done a better job of hiring more well-rounded employees she wouldn't have been forced to rearrange her world so as to accommodate their imperfections; that, in the end, capitalizing on what is unique about each employee is not the first skill of the great manager, but rather is the last resort of the manager who doesn't know how to pick the right people.

This is not at all the case. Great managers do not capitalize on each person's uniqueness because they made the mistake of hiring mediocre employees. They capitalize on each person's uniqueness because, even when they are blessed with the most talented of employees, they know that the power of individualization is extraordinarily far-reaching. I've characterized Michelle's successes as quintuple wins, but this is actually an underestimation. Here are a few other possible wins.

First, and most obviously, capitalizing on each person's uniqueness saves you time. Even the most talented employees are not perfectly well-rounded. The inefficient manager is one who fights against these imperfections and tries to eradicate them. Michelle could have spent untold hours coaching and cajoling Jeffrey to get better at remembering customers' names, smiling at them, and making friends with them, but she would have had little improvement to show for her efforts. Her time was much better spent determining how to change his role so that he would have to do less and less of this and more and more of those activities for which he displayed some natural ability. Likewise, she could have devoted significant energy to counselling Genoa on how to get along better with her immediate supervisor. But why bother when a positive outcome was by no means assured, whereas a slight reconfiguration of role and responsibility freed both employees from the friction of the relationship?

Second, finding and capitalizing on each person's uniqueness makes each person more accountable. Michelle didn't just
praise Jeffrey for his ability to execute specific assignments. Instead she challenged him to make this ability the cornerstone of
his contribution to the store. She asked him to take ownership
for this ability, to practise it, and to refine it. In simple terms,
what she was saying to Jeffrey was "If this is the best of who
you are, then I expect you to contribute and cultivate the best of
who you are each and every day." Obviously, she is sending the
same message to all of her employees. With each person feeling
the same pressure to demonstrate his or her very best, whatever
that happens to be, it's little wonder her store sustains its success month after month, year after year.

Third, capitalizing on what is unique about each person
builds a stronger sense of team. This is counterintuitive, but the
more you think about it, the more compelling it becomes. The
strongest teams are built around the concept of interdependency. "Interdependency" is a long, dry word. When you get
right down to it, what it really means is that each team member
comes to feel about every other team member, "I need you, and
I rely on you, and I value you, because you do things that I can't
do. And you feel the same about me, because I can do things you
can't do." By identifying, emphasizing, and celebrating each
person's uniqueness you, the manager, accelerate these feelings. You make people need one another. The old cliché states
that "there is no 'I' in TEAM." But as Michael Jordan was once
quoted as saying, "There is in WIN."

Finally, when you capitalize on what is unique about each
person you introduce a healthy degree of disruption into your

world. You shuffle the deck. You shuffle existing hierarchies—if Jeffrey is in charge of all resets and revisions in the store, should he now command more or less respect than an assistant manager? You shuffle existing assumptions about who is allowed to do what—if Jeffrey devises new methods of resetting an aisle, does he have to ask permission to try these out, or can he just experiment on his own? You shuffle existing beliefs about where the true expertise lies—if Genoa discovers that her way of arranging new merchandise is more appealing than the planogram sent down from Walgreens HQ, does her expertise trump the planners back at corporate, or do her insights get squashed by the experts from above?

There may be no right answers to these questions. But certainly these questions will challenge Walgreens' current orthodoxies, and, thus challenged, Walgreens will, or should, become more inquisitive, more intelligent, more vital, and more able, despite its size, to duck and weave into the future.

When you capitalize on what is unique about each person, you stimulate individual excellence. And when people excel, they not only stand out, they also stand tall. Which is to say their vision is better. Since they have come to know a particular area in great detail, within this area they are able to look around the corner and see farther, faster, sooner. Who knows what kind of disruptive discoveries they might make. Ultimately you may choose to reject their discoveries, but, as a great manager, you would be wise to keep your mind open to them.

Despite the many benefits of individualization, the sceptic will say, "Yes, but can't you take this cherishing of uniqueness too far? The point of an organization is not to give each employee the chance to express himself. The point of an organization is to fulfill its mission. In the service of this mission, you're not always going to be able to accommodate the unique needs of each particular employee."

This is one of the few instances where the sceptic is correct. History is littered with examples of people who became so fixated on their idiosyncrasies that they ceased to contribute to society and instead lapsed into eccentricity. Some of the most outlandish examples turn out to be British. In his book *An Intimate History of Humanity,* the Oxford historian Theodore Zeldin describes a couple of choice examples: "The fifth Duke of Portland, a maniac for privacy, refused to admit even his doctor into his bedroom, requiring him to make his diagnosis standing outside, questioning and taking his temperature through the medium of a valet. . . John Christie built himself his own opera house at his home, Glyndebourne, at which formal dress was required, but often wore old tennis shoes with his, liked to introduce his guests to each other by the wrong names, and died before he was able to build a cafeteria for accompanying dogs."

How can you determine whether you should continue to try to capitalize on a person's uniqueness, or whether the person's eccentricities are so extreme that you should cut your losses and find someone else for the role?

Well, since each person's situation is, by definition, unique, there isn't one answer. But there is one obvious reference point. If the person is making a significant contribution to the organization, it is often worth shuffling existing arrangements in order to accommodate his uniqueness. If he isn't, then it isn't. The point of individualizing is not to help each person bring forth his inner child, or whatever. The point is to help him contribute his utmost. If he's not contributing, stop wasting everybody's time and move him out. As a former colleague of mine liked to say, there's a fine line between a prima donna and an unemployed flake, and this line is performance.

However, while acknowledging the link between individualization and performance, great managers are intrigued by each employee's uniqueness not simply because it serves to drive performance, but also because they can't help it. This explains the heading for this section, "Great Managers Are Romantics". This is not meant to suggest that all great managers become misty-eyed during Tom Hanks/Meg Ryan movies—although they might (who didn't love *Sleepless in Seattle*?). Rather, they are Romantics in the same sense that such nineteenth-century poets as Lord Byron, Shelley, and Keats were Romantics. To cite Theodore Zeldin once more: "The Romantics claimed that each individual combines human attributes in a unique way, and that one should aim at expressing one's uniqueness in one's manner of living, just like an artist expressing himself in his creative act. The Romantic feels the individuality of other people, and he considers that individuality sacred, not because of how important or powerful its possessor is, but because it is individuality. . . [They] see in every person somebody different, as complex as a garden full of plants and a lake full of fishes, and in each plant and each fish, yet another garden and another lake."

Just as the Romantics were, great managers are fascinated by the individuality of individuals, by the subtle distinction that, while Jeffrey is bored by the generic request to straighten the store, he is fired up when presented with the specific challenge to reset the vitamin aisle. These fine shadings of uniqueness, invisible though they may be to some and frustrating to others, are to great managers as clear and as wonderful as the spectrum of colours in a rainbow. They could no more ignore them than ignore their own needs and desires.

Of course, this begs the question, Is capitalizing on a person's uniqueness a learnable skill or an innate talent? The truth is a little of each. Like all great managers, Michelle Miller has a preternatural ability to pick up on the unique style, needs, and desires of each of her people. I've chosen to emphasize what she discovered about Jeffrey and Genoa, but I should tell you that, during our time together, she made me see many different employees through her eyes, and her descriptions were as vivid and as precise as those of the characters in a Dickens novel. This ability is so pronounced in Michelle that I'd wager that she would be able to identify, keep distinct, and capitalize on the uniqueness of upwards of forty or fifty direct reports.

If, as I described in the previous chapter, an instinct for coaching is the first talent required of great managers, the ability to perceive individual differences is the second. After all, if you can't see the uniqueness in a person, it's mighty hard to capitalize on it.

How can you tell whether you (or someone else) possess some measure of this talent? The simplest way is to ask yourself some questions, such as:

- How should you motivate an employee?

- How often should you check in with an employee?
- What is the best way to praise an employee?
- What is the best way to teach an employee?

Pause for a moment to think through your answers.

If, to each of these questions, you found yourself answering, "Well, it all depends on who the employee is," it's a good clue that you possess a certain amount of talent for individualization. This is all to the good (at least as far as your efforts as a manager are concerned). But the fact that you have it doesn't necessarily mean that you are set up to use it effectively. Indeed, given that many organizations are blind to the need to capitalize on each employee's uniqueness, it's likely that the greater part of your talent to individualize remains untapped.

Fortunately, as we shall see in the following pages, there are certain skills and insights you can learn to refine this talent and thereby solidify it as the essence of your approach to managing

## THE THREE LEVERS

*"What are the three things you need to know about a person in order to manage him or her effectively?"*

Although the Romantics were correct that each person is as "complex as a garden full of plants and a lake full of fishes, and in each plant and each fish, yet another garden and another lake," you're not going to make much headway as a manager if you become hypnotized by each person's infinite layers of uniqueness. The law of diminishing returns is at work here. At some point you'll have to rein in your investigation of a person's idiosyncrasies, gather up what you know, and figure out how to use it to help the person perform.

What is that point? Well, obviously, it will vary according to the person, but, at the very least, there are three things you need to learn about a person in order to manage him effectively, three levers that you can pull to help him perform. First, you need to learn his strengths and weaknesses; second, his triggers; and third, his unique style of learning. Identify these three levers accurately, and you'll have enough information to start playing chess.

## Strengths and Weaknesses

Asking a manager to identify a person's strengths and weaknesses is almost as elementary as asking an artist to identify the primary colours in his palette. This is not to say it's always easy to identify a person's strengths and weaknesses—in fact, given that many people are inarticulate about their own strengths and weaknesses, it can actually prove quite tricky. (We'll describe a few of the best ways to do this later.) But the advice to do so is rather straightforward. As with the artist and his colours, though, what separates the great manager from the mediocre is what he decides to do with these strengths and weaknesses once he's identified them.

The mediocre manager believes that most things are learnable and therefore that the essence of management is to identify each person's weaker areas and eradicate them.

The great manager believes the opposite. He believes that the most influential qualities of a person are innate and therefore that the essence of management is to deploy these innate qualities as effectively as possible and so drive performance.

Clearly, these beliefs create diametrically opposed approaches to management. The mediocre manager tends to be a little suspicious of people's strengths and fears that his people will become overconfident and arrogant. Consequently, he thinks that it is his duty to give each employee clear and accurate feedback about her weaknesses. His goal is to get each employee to take full responsibility for her areas of weakness so that she can apply herself to plugging these gaps. If and when an employee experiences some measure of success, the mediocre manager makes it a point to praise her hard work at confronting and overcoming her weaknesses.

The great manager acts very differently. He is not preoccupied with concerns about overconfidence. Instead, his greatest fear is that he will fail to help each person turn her innate talents into performance. As such he spends most of his time either challenging each employee to identify, practise, and refine her strengths, or, as Michelle Miller did, rearranging the world so as to take full advantage of those strengths. If and when the person succeeds, the great manager doesn't praise her hard work. Instead he tells her that she succeeded precisely because she has become so good at deploying her strengths.

Great managers do all this instinctively, but recent research confirms the wisdom of their instincts. For example, conventional wisdom tells us that self-awareness is a good thing; that people who have a realistic assessment of their strengths and weaknesses outperform those whose assessments are inflated; that, in short, unrealistic self-confidence leads to a fall. Hence the widespread use of 360-degree surveys to reveal to an employee how her peers, direct reports, and supervisor perceive her performance.

In this case, however, conventional wisdom is misguided. Current research suggests that accurate self-awareness rarely drives performance, and that in many circumstances, it actively retards performance. Only *self-assurance* drives performance, even when this self-assurance turns out to be unrealistic.

For example, researchers from a number of different universities have conducted studies in which they asked children from lower socioeconomic segments of society whether they thought they were likely to get into college. Objective data revealed that these children, with their disadvantaged status, actually had a slim chance of making it through high school, let alone gaining admission to college. Those children who thought they didn't have the ability to go to college, who were, in this sense, *realistic* in their self-assessment, ended up performing in line with their assessment—very few of them made it to college. Conversely, a significant percentage of those children who thought they had what it took to make it to college, who were *unrealistically* optimistic, actually wound up getting in. Realism hindered performance, whereas unrealistic self-assurance fostered it.

Researchers discovered the same finding when studying the link between social anxiety and social activity (which they posited as a desirable behaviour). They selected two groups of people, one a group of anxious and nervous types, the other more socially active, and measured the social skills of each group—how well did they remember names, how comfortable were they at introducing themselves to a stranger, and so on. To their surprise they found virtually no difference whatsoever in the actual skill levels of each group.

They then asked the members of each group to rate themselves on their social skills. Here the two groups differed dramatically. The anxious, nervous group assessed their skill levels accurately, whereas the more socially active group gave themselves inflated ratings. They thought they had more skills than they actually did. As with the children, though, their overly positive view of themselves didn't trip them up; instead, it pushed them to apply the skills they imagined they possessed.

Here again, realistic self-assessment retarded performance, while unrealistic self-assessment stimulated it.

Given that most organizations make a virtue of accurate self-assessment and dedicate their performance appraisal process to giving you a full and accurate picture of your strengths and weaknesses, the discovery that realism doesn't drive performance may seem topsy-turvy to you. However, lest you get the impression that blithe overconfidence is the secret to a person's success, let's consider one other recent finding.

Lately a great deal of time and money has been focused on redesigning educational material in order to make it more relevant and accessible for kids—less boring tests, more fun-but-educational television shows and video games. The underlying theory is that children will learn more from this kind of edutainment, as it's sometimes called. The widespread belief in this theory explains why *Sesame Street* is still going strong and why such newcomers as *Blue's Clues* and *Dora, the Explorer* prove so popular with both children and parents.

Unfortunately, it's not true. Fabulous as these programmes are (at least according to two young critics in my house), they don't seem to teach very much. In the *Journal of Educational Psychology,* in a paper titled "Television Is 'Easy' and Print Is 'Tough' ", researchers revealed their finding that "children . . . invested high cognitive effort and learned much from instructional media they considered difficult," i.e., written tests, "but invested less effort and learned less from the same information conveyed by media they believed to be easy," i.e., television shows.

One implication for you, the manager, is that if you want your people to knuckle down and apply themselves, you've got to make them believe that the tasks they are engaged in are challenging. You've got to imbue them with a healthy degree of awe for the difficulty of their assignments. If you let them think it'll be a cakewalk, you'll slow both their learning and their achievement.

This appears to contradict the previous findings linking inflated self-assurance to performance, but it actually doesn't. Here's how all these findings can be reconciled and, in so doing, can show you how to manage your people more effectively.

As the research reveals, people who have a slightly unrealistic confidence in their abilities outperform those whose self-assessments are more realistic. These overconfident optimists are also more persistent and more resilient when faced with obstacles—"I'm not giving up now because deep down I believe I have what it takes to succeed." So if you want a person to achieve his utmost and to persist in the face of resistance, reinforce his belief in his strengths, even overemphasize these strengths, give him an almost unreasonable confidence that he has what it takes to succeed. Your job is not to provide him with a realistic picture of the limits of his strengths and the liability of his weaknesses—you're a manager, not a therapist. Your job is to get him to perform.

Stated more bluntly, your job is to build his self-assurance, not his self-awareness. So, having defined the outcomes you want, inflate his belief in his strengths and then challenge him to figure out the best way to use his strengths to achieve the outcomes.

So far, so good. But how can you guard against the possibility that this strengths-based puffing-up will lead him to waltz into work with all the nonchalance of a three-year-old watching Elmo? Well, don't try to bring him down to earth by detailing his many weaknesses and telling him he'd better set about fixing them. At times this may be tempting, particularly with your most arrogant prima donna, but you must resist. You will be fuelling his self-doubt, and although self-doubt may occasionally serve a purpose, it's unlikely to spawn excellent performance.

Instead, to combat nonchalance, build up the size of the challenge. Having detailed the outcomes you want, tell him how hard it's going to be to achieve them. Emphasize their scope, their complexity, their "no one has ever pulled this off before" quality. Do whatever you can to get his attention and make him take his challenge seriously.

In short, the state of mind you should try to create in him is one where he has a *fully realistic assessment of the difficulty of the challenge ahead of him, and, at the same time, an unrealistically optimistic belief in his ability to overcome it.* The more skilled you become at creating this state of mind in each of your people, the more effective a manager you will be.

And if this person succeeds, should you praise him for his hard work or for his unique strengths? Always the latter. Tell him he succeeded because his strengths carried the day. Even if other, external factors played a significant role in his success, still explain his success as a function of his strengths. It doesn't matter if this assessment is, in part, an illusion, because it is an illusion that will serve to create a better reality. It will reinforce the self-assurance he needs to be resolute and persistent when taking on the next challenge, and the next.

And should he fail? Assuming the failure is not attributable to factors beyond his control, always explain failure as a lack of effort, even if this is only partially accurate. This explanation will avoid infecting him with self-doubt, and instead will give him something to control, something to work on as he strives to succeed with the next assignment.

And should he fail repeatedly? Repeated failure will require different interventions entirely. Repeated failure reveals that he has weakness where the role requires strength. What should you do then?

Should you ignore weaknesses? Obviously not. Each person struggles with certain aspects of his role, and left unaddressed, these weaknesses can potentially undermine his strengths and diminish or even derail his performance entirely. So, when confronted by a person's weakness, don't close your eyes to it in some power-of-positive-thinking hope that it will just disappear. Instead, try this sequence of strategies.

First, figure out whether the person's struggles are being caused by his lack of skills or knowledge, rather than by a lack of talent. This is actually quite easy to do. Simply provide him with training in the skills or the knowledge he lacks, allow him some time to incorporate these into his behaviour, and then see whether his performance improves. If it does, your problem is solved. If it doesn't, logic now forces you to conclude that he is struggling because he is missing certain talents, in which case no amount of skills or knowledge training is going to "fix" him. You're going to have to try something else to manage around this weakness and neutralize it.

So, on to the second strategy. Can you find him a partner, someone whose talents are strong in precisely those areas where his are weak? Partnership is not the crutch of the imperfect, but the secret of the successful. Perhaps it can be made to work for your struggling employee.

And should the perfect partner prove hard to find, try this third strategy. Insert into the employee's world a technique or trick that accomplishes through discipline what the employee is unable to accomplish through instinct. Later in the book, we'll meet a very successful screenwriter/director who excels at many aspects of his work, but who struggles with telling other professionals, such as composers or directors of photography, that their work is not up to snuff. However, he isn't paralyzed by this lack of talent for confrontation. Instead, whenever direct confrontation is called for, his technique is to imagine what the "god of art" would want and to use this imaginary god as a source of strength. In his mind, he is now no longer imposing his own opinion on his colleague that he thinks the work isn't good enough. Instead, what he is saying, to himself, as much as to his colleague, is that an authoritative third party, the god of art, has decided that the work isn't good enough and that consequently both of them will now have to knuckle down and make it better.

This is a neat mental trick that seems to work for him. It'll be worth your while trying to devise something equally neat to compensate for your employee's weakness.

The final strategy is the most extreme. If skills and knowledge training produce no improvement, if complementary partnering proves impractical, if no nifty technique can be found, you are going to have to rearrange the employee's working world so that his weakness is no longer in play. You're going to have to do what Michelle Miller did and reassign roles and responsibilities so that your employee's weakness is made irrelevant. This strategy will require of you first the creativity to envision a more effective arrangement, and second the courage to force it through in the face of existing arrangements, but, as Michelle found, this creativity and courage can pay significant performance dividends.

To show you what these four strategies look like in real life, consider these examples from the world of Judi Langley, one of the best managers I have ever interviewed. Wherever her travels have taken her—from the Limited, to the Gap, to Banana Republic, to her current role as vice president of merchandising for the women's clothing retailer Ann Taylor—Judi has excelled at finding and capitalizing on the uniqueness of each of her people. Such is her genius for individualization that no matter what the nature of the performance problem, she still manages to find a way to manoeuvre around it and set the employee up for success.

Take her employee Claudia. Claudia is one of Judi's merchandising managers, and as such she is responsible for straddling the worlds of creativity and commerce. On one side, she has to work hand in glove with the clothing designers to craft a line of clothes that fit the brand goals of Ann Taylor; on the other, she has to know enough about the realities of retail to determine which of the designs will sell in volume and which won't. If she and the designers lose sight of the client, she could wind up green-lighting clothes that are beautiful but too limited in their appeal to sell well. But if she focuses too narrowly on high-volume merchandise she could miss out on special items that have low volume potential but high brand appeal for a new client.

Over the last few years, Claudia has proven her ability in both of these roles. She is intense, analytical, personable enough to get along to with both designers and the rest of the cross-functional team, and above all, supremely committed to the brand.

But despite these qualities, Judi received feedback that Claudia's colleagues in production were struggling with her. Apparently, Claudia's analytical mind and exhaustive command of detail were frustrating them. They were starting to feel that no matter what answer or solution they brought to the table, Claudia would pose another question or propose another idea they would then have to research. She was wearing them out.

To combat this situation, Judi opted for the first strategy: get Claudia the knowledge she needs and see if things improve.

And happily, they did. Judi and Claudia agreed that Claudia should go to Asia on what is called a costing trip. For the first time in her career Claudia was given the chance to tour the factories, meet the owners, and become directly involved in the price negotiations for each item. This hands-on experience in hammering out the deals with the factories and the overseas office gave her an appreciation for the challenges production faced, and enabled her to become much more insightful and supportive when she returned home to New York.

"Claudia and her production partner found a mutual respect," Judi says. "Waiting in airports between countries, they had honest conversations about what was frustrating in Claudia's relentless questioning, and how her production partner could prepare and challenge Claudia to cut bait and finalize her decision without driving each other crazy. In line reviews with the designers, Claudia could now represent the production information with confidence instead of challenging it. She'd say stuff like 'This year our waistband is going to cost us a dollar fifty, whereas last year we only invested fifty cents in our waistband construction. Personally I think this increased investment is worth it in our career line, but I'd love design's support to do something simpler at opening price points.'"

While this improvement represented a victory for both Judi and Claudia, another challenge remained. Claudia's analytical mind created in her an overpowering need to know. This need was so strong that, if she happened to uncover information before Judi could review it with her, she would become intensely frustrated. Given the speed with which decisions were made and Judi's crazy meeting schedule, this happened quite frequently. Judi was concerned that Claudia's frustration was an unsettling distraction for her and the team, not to mention that it was getting her an undeserved reputation as a malcontent.

An average manager might have lectured Claudia on the need to rein in her need to know, but Judi, as any great manager would, realized that this "weakness" was actually an aspect of her greatest strength, her analytical mind. Claudia would never be able to "rein it in", at least not for long. Instead, Judi looked for a strategy to honour and support Claudia's need to know, while at the same time channeling it more productively. This turned out to be a combination of strategies two and three. I'm going to quote her at length here because her explanation does a better job than I could of showing you the subtle but practical thought processes of a great manager.

"We worked out a little technique where I would serve as her information partner. I didn't want to become an enabler of some overactive desire of hers, you know what I mean? But on the other hand I realized, wow, she really feels good when she's in command of all the information, and she's very helpful in giving a reaction to things, you know, when you run it by her. So, I thought, What's a reasonable amount of communication pressure to put on myself? 'Cause I'm not going to sign up for something and then disappoint her.

"So we did a couple of things. We set up regular 'touch bases' at the beginning and end of each week, so now she knows that anything I can't tell her on the fly, we will catch in one of those two nets. Also, I committed to voice-mailing her at the end of every day with a brief update of everything I knew about that I thought she would want to know.

"And just doing those two things solved the problem completely. It paced her, you see. It managed her expectations and calmed her down. It enabled me to say to her, 'Claudia, you know we're going to meet at the beginning and the end of each week, but if somebody gets to you before I do, because I'm in back-to-back meetings or something, you can't be disappointed. You can't be bummed at me. You have to expect that sometimes.' Or I'd say, 'If you want to come to this meeting, fine, but your time probably doesn't permit that. So let me represent you at the meeting, and then I'll pull it all together at the end of the day and voice-mail it to you.' Just stupid little things like that really helped."

"Stupid little things like that" always seem to help when you're trying to figure out how to limit the downside of an employee's potentially damaging quirk.

In another case, none of the first three strategies applied. Allison was a designer in Women's at Banana Republic. Her strength was her ability to see the next trend just starting to happen, and her first prototype of the idea was always, in the lingo of the trade, "fashion forward". "She was just so good," Judi says, "at shopping for and identifying the fashion direction of the moment before it hit anyone else's radar. It was her unique gift."

Her weakness was her intense annoyance with the compromises required to make her designs commercial. Product line review meetings where style changes are discussed with the merchants are difficult for any designer, but for Allison, they seemed almost physically painful. She would proudly display her new denim design, the merchant would argue that the design should be modified to fit more body types, Allison would fire back that these changes would ruin the integral design aesthetic, and up the argument would spiral. Stalemate. Inefficiency. Bad feelings all around.

Judi tried a variety of techniques to manage the situation.

Flattery: "Allison, the only way your beautiful clothes are going to be seen by customers is if we get consensus on the fit and get it in the store." But Allison was too smart for flattery.

Cold, hard facts: "Michelle owns the fit decision in San Francisco. If we make this too hard, she has every right to go the decision alone." This just sounded like a threat.

She even tried the empathic approach: "Allison, why are you feeling so frustrated? Is there not enough of a fashion component? Is a little fit change such a big deal?" Judi could see on her face that yes, it was a big deal.

With Allison's DNA proving resistant to rewiring, Judi found herself spending more and more of her time explaining and apologizing for Allison's behaviour. At that point, many managers would probably have lost patience with her and offered her some kind of ultimatum: either play nicer with others or leave the team. But Judi was loath to lose someone with such a gift for fashion foresight. She would try one last strategy to alleviate the frustrations.

"I thought to myself, She's got such an incredible talent for fashion foresight, why not figure out how to focus her time so that she doesn't have to sit in too many merchant sessions where she gets so frustrated? I can take her place on these teams anyway, getting her buy-in ahead of time. And instead of these team meetings, she'll spend more time pushing the envelope forward in terms of design.

"So that's what we did. And it worked great. Allison was liberated to focus on what she loved, and had far less frustration in her day. The merchants and I understood each other and had little trouble negotiating the business decisions."

Obviously, things don't always play out quite so perfectly. Sometimes your employee will resist moving into the new role you have crafted for her. She may see it as a demotion, or perhaps she remains unaware that she has the weakness you are working so hard to manage around, and so she cannot "own" the need to redefine her responsibilities. Whenever this happens, the temptation is to confront her with ever more vivid examples of her weakness in hopes that she will finally get the point.

Try to resist this temptation. If you must confront her with something, confront her with measured proof of her poor performance. Don't delve into the intricacies of the weaknesses that caused it. Detailed descriptions of weaknesses tend not to be very persuasive, and besides, as we saw earlier, your job is to increase her self-assurance, not her self-awareness, because the more self-assured she is, the more productive and resilient she will be in the future. So if she resists your initial attempts to redesign her role, describe vividly the particular strengths you've seen that will enable her to excel at the new role. Help her see why these strengths mesh with the new set of responsibilities. Challenge her to put these strengths to work. And then, once she's in the role, let her excellent performance do the persuading for you.

And if she resists to such an extent that you can't even get her to try out the new role? Well, at this point, in the words of Jack Welch, it is probably time to allow her to pursue her career opportunities elsewhere.

## Triggers

After years of research, I suppose I should be immune to such similarities by now, but I continue to be intrigued when I see great managers in entirely different fields respond to an employee, a situation, or a question in exactly the same way. To introduce the concept of triggers, consider this example.

Not long ago I happened to be visiting a boron mine a couple of hours south of Death Valley (more on why in the next chapter), and while I was there I got a chance to interview their best mine supervisor, Russ Wooleford. Russ certainly looks the part. He is a big, ruddy walrus of a man, with load-bearing shoulders and hardscrabble hands. But his manner is calm, almost gentle, his voice light, and as he speaks I notice a slight lisp—when he introduces himself I misunderstand and wind up calling him "Ruff". He is too polite to correct me.

Toward the end of the interview, I ask him how he gets the most out of his people, and he replies: "Well, you've got to find out what their triggers are. Like, I had this one worker, he was so meek he'd get clammy whenever I talked to him. He was a good worker and all, reliable, safe, but boy, I had to treat him with kid gloves in order to get the best out of him. I had another guy, on the same shift as it happens, who was just the most confrontational SOB I've ever worked with. He wouldn't get off his ass unless I was shouting at him. He loved it so much I swear he would search me out just to fight with me. I guess he thought I wasn't doing my job if I wasn't on his case."

This answer sparked a memory of another answer, which, for some reason, has stayed with me for more than a decade.

Back in 1991, Bill Parcells coached the New York Giants to victory in the Super Bowl. In the postgame press conference a reporter asked, "You used two quarterbacks throughout the season, Phil Simms and Jeff Hostetler. How did you keep them both so productive and avoid a distracting quarterback controversy?" To which Coach Parcells replied, "I figured out how to trip each one's trigger. Phil Simms is a talented quarterback, but he needs to be challenged. You've got to get in his face all the time or he doesn't give his all. Jeff's very different. If you raise your voice with him even one tone, he'll close you out. What works with him is a quiet word in his ear."

Legendary Manchester United manager, Alex Ferguson needed the most acute "trigger-awareness" when the club took on the famously volatile French striker, Eric Cantona. As soon as Cantona arrived at the club, Ferguson resolved to ignore the media image of the supposed *enfant terrible* and communicated regularly and sympathetically with him. He got to know that Cantona, in contrast to his outwardly arrogant persona, possessed a fragile confidence, which at times needed bolstering by simply telling him he was special.

After the infamous incident between Cantona and a Crystal Palace fan, which resulted in a lengthy ban, there was a real danger that Cantona would have to leave the club and return to France for good. Ferguson went to enormous trouble to convince his star player to stay, famously pulling off the feat in a Paris restaurant specially closed for the meeting between the two men. By treating him with respect and showing him how much he and the club valued him, Ferguson managed to convince Cantona that, no matter what, he would have people who cared for him and would support him.

Great managers, like Russ Wooleford, Bill Parcells and Alex Ferguson are always on the lookout for each person's triggers. They know that a person's strengths, although powerful in their own right, will require precise triggering to keep them switched on. Squeeze the right trigger and the person will be more likely to push himself harder and to persevere in the face of resistance. Squeeze the wrong one—raise your voice at Jeff Hostetler, for example—and the person may well shut down.

The tricky thing about triggers is that they come in a myriad of forms. One employee's trigger might be tied to time of day—he is such a night owl that only after 3:00 p.m. do his strengths kick in. Another employee's trigger might be tied to time with you, the boss—even though he's worked with you for more than five years, he still needs you to check in with him every day or he starts to feel ignored. Another employee's trigger might be just the opposite—independence. She's worked for you for only six months, but if you check in with her even once a week she thinks you're micromanaging her.

Sometimes you'll trigger an employee's strengths simply through the way you present a challenge. Here's Steve Hurst, one of the consumer electronic retailer Best Buy's most successful regional managers, describing three of his store managers: "James is such a hard-driving go-getter that my goals for him have to be so challenging, so stretching that even I think they're unrealistic. But he seems to respond to these kinds of goals. He likes being hit by the goal equivalent of a two-by-four. Gil is a more analytical type. He likes to figure his way in, out, and around a problem. So if I want him to go in a certain direction, I have to throw him a rational, analytical lifeline and let him reel himself in. With Farid, I've found that a little gentle sarcasm works best, like 'Go ahead and set that goal for yourself, Farid, but I'm not sure you're going to reach it.' He works hardest when he's trying to prove me wrong."

Of all the different types of triggers, by the far the most powerful is the recognition trigger. Most managers know that employees respond well to recognition. Great managers refine and extend this insight. They realize that each employee is playing to a slightly different audience. If you are to excel as a manager you must be able to match the employee to the audience he values the most.

For example, one employee's audience might be his peers—the best way you can praise him is to stand him up in front of them and publicly celebrate his achievement. Another's might be you—the most powerful recognition for him will be a one-on-one conversation with you where you describe in detail why he is such a valuable member of the team. Another employee might define himself by his expertise, and so his most memorable recognition will be some form of professional or technical qualification. Still another might value feedback only from customers, in which case a picture of her with her best customer or a letter written to her by this customer will be the best recognition she has ever received.

Obviously, given how much personal attention it requires,

tailoring praise to fit the person is mostly the manager's responsibility. However, this doesn't mean that organizations are completely off the hook. With a little thought, there's no reason why a large organization couldn't take this individualized approach to recognition and scale it across every employee.

Of all the companies I've encountered, HSBC–North America has done the best job of this. Each year they present their top performers with Dream Awards. As most companies do, HSBC uses objective performance criteria to determine who should receive these awards. What makes their approach so different, and so powerful, is that each winner receives a unique award. During the year, the company sends out a survey to every employee asking them to identify what prize they would like to receive if they should win. The prize value is capped at $10,000, and it cannot be redeemed as cash, but other than these two restrictions, each employee is free to pick whatever prize he wants. Then, at the end of the year, after the winners have been identified by their performance, HSBC cross-references each winner to the prize he identified, shoots a video explaining why he won and why he selected his particular prize, and, in the big Dream Awards gala, plays the video and awards the prize.

You can imagine the impact of these personalized prizes. It's one thing to be brought up on stage and given yet another plaque and another obscure Lucite trophy. It's another thing entirely when, in addition to public recognition of your performance, you receive college tuition for your child or your new kitchen or the Harley-Davidson motorcycle you've always dreamed of or—the prize everyone at the company still talks about—the airline tickets to fly you and your family back to Mexico to visit the grandmother you haven't seen in ten years.

## *Style of Learning*

The third thing you need to know about a person is his particular style of learning. It would be so much easier for managers if everyone learned in exactly the same way, but of course they don't. Each person's mental receiver is tuned to a distinct frequency. Broadcast your message on the wrong frequency, and no matter how sage your advice or how carefully crafted your lesson plan, it won't be heard.

Although there are as many styles of learning as there are learners, a review of adult-learning theory reveals that three predominate. Each of the three will require a slightly different coaching technique from you. I am not suggesting that these three styles are mutually exclusive. Certain employees may rely on a combination of two or perhaps even all three styles. Nonetheless, keep your ear attuned to each of these three styles and you should be able to focus your coaching with greater accuracy.

First, there's **Analyzing.** Claudia from Ann Taylor is an Analyzer. She understands a task by taking it apart, examining its elements, and reconstructing it piece by piece. And since in her eyes, every single piece is important, she craves information. She needs to know all there is to know about a subject before she can begin to feel comfortable with it.

If she doesn't feel she has enough information she will dig and push until she gets it. She will read the assigned reading.

She will attend the required classes. She will take good notes. She will practise.

The best way to teach an Analyzer is to give her ample time in the classroom. Role-play with her. Post-mortem with her. Break her performance down into its component parts so that she can then carefully build it back up into a total performance. Always allow her time to prepare.

Remember, the Analyzer hates mistakes. A cliché about learning is that "mistakes fuel learning", but for the Analyzer this just isn't true. In fact the reason she prepares so diligently is to minimize the possibility of mistakes. So whatever you do, don't expect her to learn much by throwing her into the middle of a new situation and telling her to wing it.

The second dominant learning style is **Doing.** And in direct contrast to the Analyzer, the absolute best way to teach a Doer is to throw him in the middle of a new situation and tell him to wing it. The most powerful learning moments for the Analyzer occur prior to the actual performance, whereas for the Doer they occur *during* the performance. The dead ends, the trials and the errors are all integral parts of his learning process.

Jeffrey, the Goth rocker from Michelle Miller's store, is a Doer. He learns the most in the act of figuring things out for himself. For him preparation is a dry, uninspiring activity. Only the task itself, with its inherent possibility of real failure or real success, is intense enough to get him to concentrate and to apply himself.

If you want a Doer to learn, do not ask him to role-play with you. Role-playing is fake and therefore uninteresting to him. Instead pick a task within his role that is simple but real, give him a brief overview of the outcomes you want, and then get out of his way. Once he has figured out how to complete this simple task, gradually increase the level of each task's complexity until he has mastered every aspect of his role. Sure, he may make a few mistakes along the way, but for the Doer, mistakes are indeed the raw material for learning.

In one sense Doers can be frustrating students because they won't give your advice much credence. They have to experience a bad or good outcome themselves before they believe that it's true. But in another sense, they are wonderful to have around. They will always be the first to jump into a new challenge and attack it with spirit.

Finally, there's **Watching,** or to use the more technical term, "imitation". Watchers won't learn much if you break a task down into its component parts and ask them to practice each part or if you ask them to role-play with you. Since most formal training programmes incorporate both of these elements, Watchers are often viewed as rather poor students.

They may be poor students, but they aren't necessarily poor learners. Watchers can learn a great deal, but only when they are given the chance to see the total performance. Studying the individual parts of a task is about as meaningful for them as studying the individual pixels of a digital photograph. For them what's important is the context of each pixel, its position relative to all the others, and they can see this, they can "get" this, only when they view the completed picture.

As it happens, this is the way I learn. Years ago, when I first began interviewing, I struggled to learn the skill of dictating a report on a person after I had interviewed him. I understood all the required steps, but I couldn't seem to put them all together.

A single report, which some of my colleagues would knock out in an hour, would take me the better part of a day.

Then one afternoon, as I was staring morosely into my Dictaphone, I overheard the voice of the analyst next door. He was talking so rapidly that my initial thought was that he was on the phone. Only after a few minutes did I realize that he was dictating a report. This was the first time I had heard someone else "in the act". I'd seen the finished report, after the tape had been transcribed—in fact I'd seen countless reports, since reading the reports of others was the way we were supposed to learn—but I'd never actually heard another analyst in the act of creation. And for me it was a revelation. I suddenly saw how everything should come together into a coherent whole. I remember picking up my Dictaphone, mimicking the cadence and I think even the accent of my neighbour, and feeling the words begin to flow.

If you're trying to teach a Watcher, by far the most effective technique is to get her out of the classroom, take her away from the manuals, and make her ride shotgun with one of your most experienced performers.

## THE MOST USEFUL QUESTIONS

*"How can you identify these levers?"*

Strengths and weakness, triggers, and unique style of learning—these are the three things you must know about a person in order to manage him effectively. But how can you identify them?

Well, obviously there's no substitute for observation. The great manager spends a good deal of time outside his office, walking around, watching each person's reactions, listening, taking mental notes about what each person is drawn to and what each person struggles with. Alison Fedeli, the manager of Wellington Hospital's 27-person physiotherapy unit in London, describes the power of observation this way: "I think all the time people are telling you things. They're showing you who they are in small ways. The ones who don't want to sign in on time. The ones that don't finish their notes. The ones that are always there at the end of the day. The ones that . . . well, different things. People are telling you things all the time. And I think you've got to listen and watch out and observe that." So, yes, get out of your office and observe.

There's also value in having your employees take certain personality-type tests such as StrengthsFinder, Myers-Briggs, Kolbe, or DISC. The results of these tests, although quite complex, can provide a structured framework and, most important, a common language for identifying how one person differs from another.

But, initially, the best way to identify these three levers is to ask a few simple questions and to listen carefully to the answers. Of all the questions I've experimented with, these five have proven to be the most revealing.

For strengths:

1. What was the best day at work you've had in the last three months?
   - What were you doing?
   - Why did you enjoy it so much?

For weaknesses:

2. What was your worst day at work in the last three months?
   - What were you doing?
   - Why did it grate on you so much?

For triggers:

3. What was the best relationship with a manager you've ever had?
   - What made it work so well?

4. What was the best praise or recognition you've ever received?
   - What made it so good?

And for unique style of learning:

5. When in your career do you think you were learning the most?
   - Why did you learn so much?
   - What's the best way for you to learn?

I recommend asking these questions of each new recruit. You can also ask them of each existing employee at the beginning of your financial year. This mini-interview will take only about half an hour, but it should be a rich half hour. Ask these five questions, listen closely, and then act on this information in the same way that Michelle, Judi, Russ, and Alison did, and you will see extraordinary results. You will discover the power of capitalizing on what is unique about each of your people.

# CHAPTER 4

# The One Thing
# You Need to Know:
# Great Leading

## A LEADER WINS OUR LOYALTY

*"What did Giuliani say to calm our fears?"*

During the long day of September 11, 2001, all of us caught in New York City became frightened; as frightened, perhaps, as we have ever been. I was living down on Tenth Street with my wife and six-month-old son, just a mile from the Trade Center towers, and, as usual, that morning I had taken the subway up to my offices in a high-rise on Forty-ninth and Sixth. In the elevator someone told me that a plane had crashed into the World Trade Center, and by the time I reached my office the second plane had hit. When I turned on my television the screen was filled with a close-up helicopter shot of black and gold oil flames.

My assistant, Danielle, ran in crying. Her husband, an IT consultant, happened to be working at the Trade Center complex that day. She had gotten a garbled message from him on her cell phone, something about trying to get out of the buildings, and then they'd lost contact. As we were deciding what to do, the first reports came in that yet another plane had crashed into the Pentagon, and, quite soon after, the sirens in our building sounded the evacuation order and we found ourselves tramping down the stairwells to the street.

We stood around in the crowds waiting for Danielle's husband. She thought he might have said that he would be making his way up to our offices, so our plan was to hang around until he arrived. An hour went by. The crowd grew larger as more buildings emptied their people onto the street. Word spread that other planes had been hijacked and that no one knew where they were. We kept looking up. Then a murmur through the crowd: one of the towers had fallen. So strange. Only one tower now. A little while later, the second fell too. No more towers at the tip of Manhattan.

The felling of the second tower spurred the crowd. It began to disperse, each person anxious now to get moving, to get home, to get away from the tall buildings. I began to think that I would have to leave Danielle and seek out my own family, when suddenly, one of many small miracles that day, her husband walked out of the crowd. Having escaped the World Trade Center area, he had spent the last two hours walking uptown. I left them to each other and began my trek down Sixth Avenue toward home.

It was an eerie scene, as I imagine the aftermath of a coup to be. I remember that the tide was against me, everyone trudging silently uptown, but I made good progress because there was no traffic. On every corner I had to push through a knot of people clustered around the open doors of a parked car or truck, all craning in to listen to the radio, and it seemed like every tenth person was covered in a fine white dust. On every face was fear.

If the walk down Sixth Avenue unnerved me, finding my family safe only increased my worry. Seeing them reminded me of all that I had to lose, and so for the rest of the day, I, like most of New York, sat stunned, alone in my thoughts, frightened for myself and for my family, scared for our future.

The old maxim in psychology tells us that if you know someone's fear you will know their need. New Yorkers are a notoriously independent-minded bunch, but it seemed as though on that day we were all feeling the same fear. At that moment, during the terror of the first day, what we needed was someone to soothe our fear. We needed empathy. And improbably, we found it in the person of our mayor, Rudy Giuliani.

I say improbably because Mayor Giuliani was known more for his combativeness than his empathy. And, despite his original great popularity as a crime fighter, in the twelve months prior to September 11, he had seemed to fall out of sync with the majority of his constituents. He had always been a polarizing figure—the fastest way to start an argument over dinner was to bring up his name—but, in the months preceding the terrorist attacks, his approval ratings had gotten worse. He had become distracted by his short-lived run for the Senate, by his public and contentious divorce, and by his fight with prostate cancer. Although I'm sure most of us sympathized with his illness, we were no longer sure that he was looking out for us, understanding us. Our loyalty was slipping away.

During 9/11, he won it back to such an extent that, if given the chance, many of us would probably have voted him into a third term. He was now greeted by standing ovations wherever he appeared. He was the world's mayor, *Time* magazine's Person of the Year, 'Sir' Rudy after his knighthood by Queen Elizabeth. Suddenly everybody loved him.

This transformation seems inevitable in hindsight, but it's easy to see how things could have worked out differently. We could have become angry that the city wasn't better prepared to handle the disaster, particularly since the World Trade Center had been attacked by terrorists once before in 1993, or we could have blamed him for the miscommunications between the fire department, the Port Authority, and the police department. We might even have complained that his agencies handled the relatives of the missing in a needlessly confusing and bureaucratic way. But for some reason we did none of these things. It's not that these issues weren't real, or that we were unaware of them at the time, it's just that we didn't feel motivated to lay them at his door.

Why? What did Mayor Giuliani do on 9/11 and the days thereafter that so transformed our feelings toward him? How did he win our loyalty so quickly and so completely? Clearly his presence at ground zero that day and his tireless efforts during the days following earned our admiration. But these alone were not enough, I think, to win our loyalty so utterly. After all, many public officials were caught at ground zero, and many worked countless hours during the rescue and recovery efforts.

Looking back, we can trace the turning point in our affections to the mayor's spontaneous answer to one question during a press conference he held late in the afternoon of the eleventh.

He was asked what he thought the final body count would be. All manner of answers would have been possible, and acceptable. He could have responded with a curt "I don't know." He could have turned to the agency heads standing behind him and passed the question off to them. He could have given a practical, dispassionate answer such as "We have not yet compiled and reconciled all the different lists. As soon as each agency submits their lists and we can compare them and reconcile them, we will release our estimate." But he didn't say any of these things. Instead he sighed, looked down, looked up, and replied: "I don't know what the final number will be, but it will be more than we can bear."

And with those eight words—"it will be more than we can bear"—he won us. He revealed himself to be a leader who understood what all of us, all twelve million diverse, disagreeable, discordant New Yorkers, were going through. He found the emotion we were all feeling—*This day is unbearable*—and he articulated it for us. And in so doing he eased our fears just a little. We didn't know what was going to happen next, but we now knew that in him we had a leader who would do right by us, who would steer us through the uncertainty. He had voiced what was in our hearts. He had spoken for us all. And we loved him for it.

This ability to cut through individual differences and fasten upon those few emotions or needs that all of us share is at the core of great leadership. This ability is called extended empathy. No matter how admirable his achievements, or how valuable his experience and expertise, when a leader lacks extended empathy, when he loses sight of those things we all share, he loses the ability to lead.

In the previous chapter, we saw that the One Thing great managers know is the need to discover what is unique about each person and to capitalize on this uniqueness. Great managers serve as intermediaries between the individual and the company, and, like all intermediaries, they perform their role well only when they perform it one on one.

Great leaders must play a different role. Their job is to rally people toward a better future, and as such, they are not intermediaries. They are instigators. Driven by their compulsion for a better future, their challenge is to do everything in their power to get other people to join together to make this future come true. So, by definition, they will perform this role well only when they find a way to make many people, regardless of each person's uniqueness, excited by and confident in this better future. If, through their words, actions, images, pictures, and scores, they can tap into those things we all share, they will succeed as leaders. If they can't, they will struggle.

So, while great managers discover what is unique about each person and capitalize on it, great leaders do the inverse. The One Thing every great leader knows he must do is:

**Discover What Is Universal
and Capitalize on It.**

The better you are able to do this, the better you will lead.

A few years ago I was working with the chief executive of a large consulting organization. During one of our many chats, I asked him what he thought the mission of his company was. Generally I am not a fan of mission statements, but in his case I felt that some time devoted to thinking about his company's core purpose would pay dividends. He pondered the question for a minute or two and then replied, "I don't think this company has one single mission. I think we have as many missions as we do employees. Some of us are driven by a desire to help our clients grow. Some are only really interested in the science part of what we do. Some of us live for making the sale. Some of us aspire to building a better society. Each of us is different, and so to identify one mission for us all would be a waste of effort."

In a sense he was right. Each of his people undoubtedly found different meaning in their work, and his recognition of this uniqueness marked him as a man of some sophistication. But nonetheless, his answer missed the mark. With its preoccupation with individual differences, and with the need to accommodate these differences, it was the answer of a manager, not a leader.

The truly effective leader, while not denying the truth that each person is different, would choose instead to focus on a separate but equally powerful truth: despite our differences, we all share a great deal. To answer my question, the effective leader would call upon his extended empathy. He would sift through his employees' many missions until he found the one they all shared. He would then reflect this shared mission back to his employees. He would pick out specific employees who today seemed to be living out this mission, and he would draw attention to them. He would paint vivid pictures of what the future would look like if this mission were made real. He would pinpoint one key metric to track everyone's progress toward this future. And by doing all this, he would reveal his understanding of us and his hope for us.

And for our part, we would start to feel a closer connection with him, a stronger sense that *his* vision was in fact *our* vision, and a growing confidence that, together, we could make this shared vision come true. He would rally us all to a better future.

## FIVE FEARS, FIVE NEEDS, ONE FOCUS

*"What are the universals of human nature?"*

Since it is so important for the effective leader to tap into those things we all share, the obvious question becomes "What, exactly, do we all share?"

If you would have asked this question of your average twentieth century anthropologist, the answer would have been, Not much. For most of the last century, anthropologists seemed to have been on a quest to prove that every society was unique, and therefore that there was no such thing as universal human nature. We shouldn't assume that aggression is a universal human trait because, look, here is the !Kung San tribe of Kalahari bushmen who are so peace-loving that they don't even have a word for murder. We shouldn't imagine that it is natural for most of us to seek marital fidelity because, look, here are the happy Samoans who have sex with many partners and who have no concept of jealousy.

However, as the century progressed and the research became less impressionistic and more disciplined, anthropologists discovered that the apparent anomalies of such societies as the !Kung San and the Samoans were just that—appearances. The truth was more prosaic, and, on a deeply human level, more familiar. In the words of the neuroscientist Steven Pinker: "Samoans may beat or kill their daughters if they are not virgins on their wedding night, a young man who cannot woo a virgin may rape one to extort her into eloping, and the family of a cuckolded husband may attack and kill the adulterer. The !Kung San . . . had been described by Elizabeth Marshall Thomas as 'the harmless people' in a book of that title. But as soon as anthropologists camped out long enough to accumulate data, they discovered that the !Kung San have a murder rate higher than that of American inner cities."

My point is not that all societies are equally violent. It is simply that, although each society embraces different customs—the British open their Christmas presents on Christmas Day, Norwegians do it on Christmas Eve, the Dutch do it on Saint Nick's Day, December 6, while the !Kung San obviously don't do it at all—there is indeed such a thing as human nature and that all societies, through their different customs and language, reflect this shared nature.

Every leader is indebted to the anthropologist Donald Brown for giving us the raw details for describing these universals of human nature. Over many years, he took it upon himself to dig up all the documented findings from every society ever studied and compile a list of human universals. By my count, he found 372 of them.

Some are quite intriguing. For example, joking is common to every society, as is tickling, and baby-talking, and the habit of sucking a wound. We all overestimate our objectivity. We all show a preference for sweets. We all create sayings that are pithy but contradictory—there is apparently a !Kung San equivalent of not only "Great minds think alike" but also "Fools seldom differ". And oddly enough, in every society we have a word for string.

Others are rather more predictable. Every society shares a fear of snakes, but not of flowers. Every society reserves a formal style of speech for special occasions. Every society includes toilet training in the education of its children. In every society, the husband is, on average, older than the wife. And every society has a word for pain.

Reading the list of universals in its entirety (which you can find in Brown's book *Human Universals*) conjures conflicting emotions. On the one hand it is depressing, yet hardly surprising, to discover that every society has weapons, rape, and murder. But on the other, it's uplifting to see that trade, toys, and the practice of taking turns all make the cut. On balance, the fact that these universals exist, both the good ones and the bad ones, is actually quite comforting. They imply that all humans share a common experience, we share common virtues and vices, and therefore that, if we are inquisitive enough, if we listen closely enough, we should be able to empathize with and understand one another. There's hope in this, I think.

For the leader, the list offers clues to the universals he can call upon to rally his followers to a better future. These universals can be readily distilled down to five, and, in the spirit of "Know someone's fear and you'll know their need", we can view them as five pairings of fears and needs. This is not to suggest that the five pairs are exhaustive. They don't capture the totality of the human experience, any more than Freud's theory of the unconscious did, or Maslow's hierarchy of needs. But they do explain why leaders are necessary. They do point to what followers require of a leader. And one of them in particular holds the secret to your effectiveness as a leader. If you can narrow your focus to this one fear and its accompanying need, you are much more likely to engender in your people the confidence to follow you into the future.

Below, I'll briefly describe the five—all of them have some relevance to your efforts at leading people—and then identify which of the five should command your greatest attention as a leader.

1. **Fear of Death (our own and our family's)—The Need for Security.** In every society we find a fear of death, rituals to commemorate death, rituals to celebrate our fertility, and prohibitions against murder and suicide. We also find, in every society, marriage, kin groupings, and a strong preference for our own children and our kin, in other words, nepotism.

   Some of our most basic needs, then, stem from our urge to secure our lives and the lives of our loved ones.

2. **Fear of the Outsider—The Need for Community.** Children in every society fear strangers. All societies live in

groups, and these groups are not based simply on family or blood ties. All societies make distinctions between those who are part of the group and those who aren't, and we are always biased in favour of the former. The chief purpose of law in all societies is to define the rules of membership for the group, and, in all societies, we devise sanctions or punishments for those who break the law, for those who, in Brown's words, "commit crimes against the collective".

The bottom line here is that we are herd animals, and we organize ourselves to keep the herd strong.

3. **Fear of the Future—The Need for Clarity.** Every society has a concept of the future. And we see its possibilities. In every society there is a word for hope and for anticipation and a capacity for, as Brown calls it, "conjectural reasoning," as in "If this happens then that will follow." But every society is also anxious about the future. We are aware that the future is unstable, unknown, and therefore potentially dangerous. We all, on some level, fear the future.

This is why, in every society, we give prestige to those people who claim to be able to predict the future. The Samoans call them seers, while we call them economists, but the point is the same—if you can help us see the future more clearly, we will give you special status. That is also why, in every society, we perform rituals to help us divine what might happen tomorrow. In Roman society this took the form of examining the liver of a goose. Today we simply read the *Financial Times,* a ritual that, although usually less messy, serves the same need for clarity.

**4. Fear of Chaos—The Need for Authority.** Two universals reveal just how much we all fear chaos. First, every society has devised its own story of how the world came to be, and in each story, in each creation myth, the world was created out of chaos. What preceded our world was never some other world, but always darkness, disorder, the void. In every society, then, the world we know is defined as the exact opposite of chaos.

Second, one of the most universal of human traits is our need to classify things. In fact, in Brown's list, by far the longest subcategory consists of those things that every society feels a need to classify. His list includes age, behavioural propensities, body parts, colours, fauna, flora, inner states, kin, sex, space, tools, and weather conditions. By imposing on the world an artificial grid that sorts things out into discrete chunks, we convince ourselves that we are keeping the chaos at bay, and that we are in control.

And out of our desire for order springs our need for authority. Having someone in charge just seems more organized than a chaotic free-for-all. Yes, this implies that we will sometimes have to submit ourselves to this person's decisions, but for the most part we are comfortable with this trade-off. Every society has a concept of the need to balance dominance with submission. And every society has a word for leader.

If you want to see this need played out in today's world, consider what happens within those countries that have recently been democratized. The populations of these countries, perhaps afraid of the chaos of multiparty democracy, tend to vote in authoritarian leaders, such as Putin in Russia, Chavez in Venezuela, Lukashenko in Belarus, and Akayev in Kyrgyzstan, and then, almost perversely, when the parliaments of these countries use referenda to try to limit the powers of the president, the people almost always vote them down—in fact, as in Kyrgyzstan in 1996, more often than not the people actually vote to extend the president's authority. The reasons why newly democratized populations persist in doing this are quite complex, but the underlying mindset is hard to deny: we dislike chaos, and so we like strong leaders.

5. **Fear of Insignificance—The Need for Respect.** Every society sees the individual person as having a worth and a value that is distinct from the group's. Every society has a word for self-image and an accompanying concept that a positive self-image is better than a negative one. Every society also espouses the not-so-obvious idea that, to a great extent, our self-image is in the hands of other people—all of us pay attention to what other people think of us. Our fear is that they will not look favourably on us or, worse still, that they will not look at us at all, that we will be insignificant in their eyes.

Thus, in every society, we find a craving for prestige and for the respect that comes with it. Indeed, throughout history, by far the most effective way to earn the respect of others was to show yourself ready to sacrifice virtually everything for the sake of pure prestige. The fact that different people craved prestige with different levels of intensity meant that some became the masters and others the serfs. The master was he who so craved significance for himself, or for those ideas he deemed worthy—his beliefs, his religion, his loyalty to tribe or to country—that he was prepared to die in pursuit of it. Those who said, "Whatever. Lighten up. I'll do it your way"—they were the serfs.

This arrangement of master and serf was, in some sense, a natural state of affairs—strength through power, in Nietzsche's famous expression—but it had an unfortunate side-effect. It created, in all societies, a shortage of respect. The masters were few but had lots of it, whereas the serfs were many and had none. So, over time, the serf searched for other avenues to get respect, and he found them in religion. Every society ever studied had some form of religion, but most have withered away. The religions that have swept the world, such as Christianity, Islam, Judaism, and Hinduism are successful precisely because they offer a way—membership in the chosen race, an afterlife, a second go-around at this life—for even people with the least earthly prestige to get respect.

Those, in brief, are the five human universals distilled from Brown's list: the need for security, for community, for clarity, for authority, and for respect. The more you understand the interplay of these fears and needs in your people, the more effective a leader you will be. However, although each is relevant to your efforts at leading, one of them demands your greatest focus.

Not the last one, the need for respect. Our need for respect is usually attended to by an intermediary, by someone who deals with people one-on-one. In the past this intermediary role was played most often by a representative of the society's religion. Your pastor, your rabbi, your priest, or your imam would meet with you and personally assure you that, although you might be low on the earthly totem pole, you were still worthy in the eyes of the Lord, and that, by following the precepts of your religion, you too had the chance to earn prestige and respect.

Today, in the world of work, this intermediary role is played most effectively by the manager, not the leader. Not everyone can or should become the chief executive, but nonetheless, each employee still has the chance to achieve nobility in his role. The great manager, by identifying each person's natural talents, those few things that make him special and different, and by challenging him to strengthen these talents with practice and discipline, shows each employee how to earn the respect that accompanies excellence. This is why great managers are so valuable, not simply within organizations, but within society at large. They provide each of us with many possible avenues to channel our craving for respect.

The fourth need, the need for authority, reveals why we crave leaders in the first place, and as such, it tells you that your role as leader is both necessary and legitimate. But it doesn't tell you much beyond that. It doesn't tell you what you should do with your leadership position once you have assumed it. It doesn't tell you what your followers want from you.

To get at this, we must turn to the remaining three needs: the need for security, the need for community, and the need for clarity. Which of these three universals should you capitalize on?

This is actually a tricky question to answer, because when push comes to shove, any one of them would work. Take the first one, our need for security. This is such a powerful, elemental need that many leaders choose to play to it. They realize, rightly, that we are more likely to have faith in a leader who promises to provide for us and to make our lives and those of our loved ones more secure. This explains why the fastest way to win a population's loyalty is to provide people with water, food, electricity, and an effective police presence; why, more often than not, leaders seek to gain support for their foreign wars by explaining them as preemptive actions to preserve national security; and why politicians, in every society, are so intent on kissing babies.

Or take the second need, the need for community. There's a reason why leaders seek out enemies, why President Bush took pains to define our common foe, his "axis of evil", why Pepsi deliberately takes aim at Coke, and why almost every leader of a social initiative resorts to describing his organization's mission in the language of war—the War on Drugs, the War on Poverty, the Fight Against Cancer. They do it because it works. Communities become strong when they know clearly what threatens them.

And what if no clear and present threat can be found? Well, many leaders are not above fabricating one. Focusing your followers on the proverbial scapegoat isn't an admirable leadership strategy, but no one ever said it wasn't effective.

Meeting either of these two needs will undoubtedly win people's loyalty. But, remember, the job of the leader is not to win people's loyalty. The job of a leader is to rally people toward a better future. Winning people's loyalty should be a means to this end, not the end itself. Of the three remaining universals, the only one that deals explicitly with the future is the third one, our fear of the future. The first two are inherently static. If you orient your leadership toward them, the best outcome you can hope for is that you will preserve the status quo. On occasion this can be a valuable outcome, but achieving it is rarely the mark of a great leader. In contrast, if you can come to grips with the third universal, if you can grapple with our fear of the future and somehow neutralize it, even turn it into something positive, you will have positioned yourself to pull off something truly significant as a leader.

Lately, many widely read books have told us that we should welcome change and embrace it as a force for good. While this advice can be momentarily uplifting, on reflection most of us realize that being fearful of change is actually quite sensible. Looking back into our prehistory, those of us who harboured no fear of the unknown, who were impulsive, impetuous, who were in the habit of wandering into dark caves, exclaiming, "Ooh, I wonder what animal lives in here!" often didn't live long enough to pass on their genes. From this angle, being a little cautious, a little frightened of the unknown is actually an adaptive human trait. Following the logic of evolution—only adaptive traits are passed on—this anxiety about the unknown must survive, to varying degrees, in all of us today. Only the naïve leader will try to dismiss it as mere weakness or to pretend that it doesn't exist. The truth is that this fear of the unknown does exist, and from an evolutionary perspective, it's good that it does.

The problem for you, the modern-day leader, is that you traffic in the unknown. All of your conversations concern the unknown, the future, and the possibilities you see there. If you are going to succeed as a leader, you simply must find a way to engage our fear of the unknown and turn it into spiritedness. If great managers are catalysts, speeding up the reaction between the individual's talents and the company's goals, then great leaders are alchemists. Somehow they are able to transform our fear of the unknown into confidence in the future.

How do they do this? Not by being passionate. A passionate leader can certainly inspire people in the moment, but passions are, by definition, volatile, unpredictable, and therefore temporary. They can wane, and so we, the followers, tend not to put our trust in them. Think back to the demise of Governor Howard Dean's presidential campaign in 2004, a campaign that began with a foundation of anger and ended after an ill-considered display of passion on an Iowa stage.

Being consistent isn't the answer either. Consistency can be comforting to us, but on some level we are aware that circumstances change, and we expect our leaders to be open-minded enough to change with them. Too much consistency from our leaders begins to seem like rigidity or lack of imagination, and thus, over time, we become suspicious of it.

By far the most effective way to turn fear into confidence is to be clear; to define the future in such vivid terms, through your actions, words, images, pictures, heroes, and scores that we can all see where you, and thus we, are headed. Of course you may have to tweak your descriptions of the future to accommodate unforeseen circumstances, but these tweaks, these small adjustments, must always be communicated with great vividness. Clarity is the antidote to anxiety, and therefore clarity is the preoccupation of the effective leader. If you do nothing else as a leader, be clear.

This doesn't mean that you must describe in precise detail all of your tactics and plans and deadlines. On the contrary, as we'll see, to keep your followers challenged and engaged you must allow them plenty of white space to invent, create, and experiment. But it does mean that your ability to be clear and your followers' feelings of confidence are causally linked. The one drives the other.

In the next section, we'll explore the four areas where your followers are crying out for clarity.

## THE POINTS OF CLARITY

*"Where are your followers crying out for clarity?"*

### 1: Who Do We Serve?

Recently I interviewed a man named Terry Leahy. Actually, the proper way to refer to him is Sir Terry Leahy—such are his contributions to British business that in 2002 he was honoured with a knighthood. Sir Terry is the chief executive of the supermarket giant, Tesco. Although Wal-Mart is the largest retailer in the world, an argument can be made that Tesco, with its 326,000 employees worldwide and its hugely successful operations in Europe and the Far East, is the best.

It wasn't always this way. For most of its fifty-year lifespan,

Tesco struggled to differentiate itself from such competitors as Sainsbury's, Safeway, and the Wal-Mart–owned ASDA stores. Today, however, Tesco is number one and pulling away. As an example, for every hundred pounds spent by U.K. consumers, Tesco gets more than twelve of them.

I started our interview with a broad question: "More than half of Tesco's square footage is outside of the U.K. With such a far-flung organization, how have you managed to keep people focused on the same priorities?"

"Well," he replied. "I began by making sure that we all knew who Tesco was trying to serve."

"Who were you trying to serve?"

"In the eighties we had lost some of our focus on who we were trying to serve. We had gone more upmarket, trying to serve the aspirational customer, and in the recession of the nineties this strategy wasn't working. So instead we returned to our heritage and to our focus on serving the working man and woman, the ordinary Joe."

"How did you decide on this?"

"Well, we interviewed upwards of two hundred thousand customers in focus groups, surveys, and the like, in the hopes of finding out what our customers wanted from Tesco."

"And did your answer emerge from this research?" I asked.

"Some of it did, I suppose, but some of it was instinct. I have a similar background to many of our core customers, a working-class background, and so I can identify with our customers' lives more readily than some. I felt that what these customers wanted from Tesco was a place that wouldn't patronize them, but that would respect them, genuinely respect them."

"What did you do to show them this respect?"

"Well, the first thing I did was dramatically increase the number of checkout lines in a Tesco. It used to be that your basic Tesco store would have limited checkout lines, and as a result there was lots of waiting around in queues. Today we've removed the queueing by installing many more checkout lines. I figured that the best way to show someone that you respect them is to respect their time. All these new checkout lines represented, as you can imagine, a huge capital investment for us, but I decided that, given who we should be trying to serve, it was the right thing to do."

Was Sir Terry right in allocating resources in this way? Was he right in focusing Tesco on serving the working man and woman who wants to find good-quality merchandise at a good price and then get out quickly and get on with their life? I don't know. The truth is, no one knows for certain, since he didn't allocate a certain number of stores to serve a different customer and then compare the results. All we can be certain of is that Sir Terry's clear answer to the question "Who do we serve?" has focused his people and enabled them to achieve lastingly positive results.

To reinforce the point that there is no right answer to the question "Who do we serve?" and that a clear answer is all that is required, one only has to look at Wal-Mart. Wal-Mart competes in exactly the same space as Tesco, and yet if you were to ask their executives "Who do you serve?" they would give a different answer from Terry Leahy's.

Last year, at the Consumer Healthcare Products Association convention, speaking before a group of executives, I followed

Doug Degn onto the podium. Doug heads up all food merchandising for Wal-Mart, and, by any measure, he has had a tremendously successful last fifteen years. Fifteen years ago he sold no food. Now he sells more food than anyone else in the world. In his speech he revealed himself to be a straight-talking, hard-working executive who was suspicious of anyone who overanalyzes an issue. Here's a typical comment from Doug: "We had one store that was selling far more fishing equipment than our projections suggested it should. Our analysts back in Bentonville were perplexed. But in the end the answer turned out to be common sense." He paused to set up the punch line. "This particular store was located very close to a large lake." Much laughter from the audience.

Despite his no-nonsense persona, he did have one little device that he used to engage the audience. Toward the end of his speech, he asked us to raise our hands if we lived paycheque to paycheque. Very few of us raised our hands. At which, he stopped his pacing, stood square on, levelled his gaze, and said: "Look, you are all welcome in our stores. Please, come into our stores. You will be treated well. But know that our stores are not designed for you. Our stores, every one of them, are designed for people who live paycheque to paycheque. Yes, you can come into our stores and find a nice gourmet pizza for six dollars and fifty cents, but I guarantee you that you will also find the best, the highest quality seventy-seven-cent pizza in the neighborhood. Everything we do, everything we buy is designed to serve those of us who live paycheque to paycheque."

Why did Wal-Mart land on this notion that they serve customers who live from one paycheque to the next? Yes, their data suggests that the lower-income customer represents the majority of their shoppers—fully 20 percent of Wal-Mart shoppers do not even have a bank account. However, Wal-Mart's history tells us that they seek to serve this customer less because their data indicate the wisdom of doing so than because Sam Walton, their founder, simply decided that this is who he wanted his company to serve. The significance here isn't that this is the right segment to serve. There is no "right" segment. The significance lies in Wal-Mart's utter commitment to serving this customer, and in the unremitting consistency with which they pursue this strategy.

And what is the benefit to knowing whom you serve? What exact advantage do the leaders of Wal-Mart, or Tesco, gain from being clear on this point? The business school explanation would be that if you, the leader, know whom you serve, you will be able to make more focused decisions about which strategies to pursue, where and how to allocate assets, and how to design your organization. All this is true, of course, which helps explain why business gurus are forever telling us to "stick to our knitting" and to embrace "the hedgehog concept".

But this explanation, accurate though it is, doesn't reach to the heart of the matter. You, the leader, must be clear about whom you are choosing to serve because we, your followers, require it of you. If we are going to follow you into the future, we need to know precisely whom we are trying to please. It is a scary thing to try to please all of the people all of the time, so, to calm our fear, we need you to narrow our focus. Tell us explicitly, vividly who our main audience is. Tell us whom we should empathize with most closely. Tell us who will be judging our success. When you do this with clarity, as Terry and Doug do, you give us confidence—confidence in our judgment, confidence in our decisions, and ultimately confidence in our ability to know where to look to determine if we have fulfilled our mission.

This advice—be clear about whom you serve—appears straightforward, but it is surprising how many leaders allow their answer to be vague, imprecise, or, most damaging of all, complex.

Consider the leaders who proclaim that their company's mission is to be the "supplier/retailer/manufacturer of choice". This pithy little phrase fits nicely on a PowerPoint slide, but what does it mean exactly? Who is doing the choosing? What criteria will they use to make their choice? How will they know if they've made a good choice? There are a great many plausible answers to these questions, and without your guidance on which answer to focus on, we, your followers, will remain anxious and ill at ease.

Then there are the leaders who announce that the mission of their organization is to return value to shareholders. The problem with this answer isn't simply that it's wrong, although it is. Shareholders are analogous to school parents: both must be satisfied if the company/school is to fulfill its mission, but both should serve as a means to the mission, rather than the mission itself. No, the chief problem with telling us that our mission is to serve the shareholder is that it leaves us at the mercy of forces beyond our control. Shareholders pay attention to stock price, and although only a few of us are up to date with such arcane macroeconomic facts as the one that says only 15 percent of stock price fluctuations can be tied to fluctuations in profitability, most of us have some awareness that stock price is influenced by many hard-to-define variables. So, when you tell us that we should seek to serve the shareholder, you are, in essence, telling us that there's not much we can do to influence the happiness of our most important audience. It's hard to imagine anything more likely to increase our level of anxiety.

Perhaps the most ineffectual answer comes from the leader who, smart as she is, sees the complexity of the world and seeks to incorporate this complexity into her public announcements of whom she is trying to serve. She is the leader of a software company who says, "We have many masters. We serve not only the end user, but also the IT vice president who controls the budget for our products." She is the leader of a pharmaceutical company who says, "We serve not only the patient, but also the doctors who prescribe our products." She is the leader of the financial services company who says, "We serve not only the individual investor, but also the independent investment advisors who have to sell our services to the individual investor."

What's ineffective about these answers is not their lack of accuracy. What's ineffective about them is that they are too accurate. There are many truths in the world, and each of these answers reaches and stretches to incorporate too many of them. The end result, although accurate, is confusing. And there is nothing more likely to foster our fear than confusion.

And yet, in defence of these leaders, the world is indeed complex. Each organization does serve many masters. How does the effective leader reconcile this truth with the need to be brilliantly clear in answering the question "Who do we serve?"

Brad Anderson's approach, although not applicable in every situation, suggests a solution: focus on one master, become expert at serving this master, and through what he calls "the power of the ripple effect", you will end up serving them all.

Brad has been with Best Buy, the electronics retailer, for over thirty years, first as a sales manager in one of their stores when the company was still called Sound of Music, and now as chief executive officer and vice chairman. In close partnership with the company's chairman and founder, Dick Schulze, he has helped guide Best Buy's transformation from a small regional retailer into a 600-store giant that dominates its category, a transformation that culminated in 2004 with *Forbes* magazine naming Best Buy its Company of the Year. This achievement is all the more remarkable because Best Buy has found a way to thrive while many of its direct competitors, such as Circuit City and the Good Guys, have felt the pressure of ever-shrinking margins and now have either been sold or struggle to make a profit. To succeed when a rising tide is raising every boat is one sort of achievement. To succeed when every other boat in the harbour is foundering on the rocks is another level of achievement entirely.

Best Buy's success, as with any example of sustained excellence, is due to a complex combination of factors, but its clear focus on serving a particular kind of customer is undoubtedly one of them. To give you some perspective on the transformation at Best Buy, bear in mind that from its founding in 1966 until 1989, Best Buy didn't devote much energy toward identifying who it was trying to serve. It was much more concerned with moving as much product as possible, and, to this end, it did what every other consumer electronics retailer was doing at the time (and some are still doing). It displayed a dizzying array of merchandise in the store, which impressed and excited the customer, but then the salespeople steered the customers toward only those products on which they knew they would make a healthy commission.

In 1989, the changes began. Dick and Brad are both good men, or, in today's parlance, principle-centred leaders, servant leaders. One example: for the last couple of years Brad quietly distributed to his employees $20 million worth of his own stock options, sent out no press release on this action, no internal memo, and became annoyed when the local Minneapolis paper sifted through Best Buy's SEC filings, discovered it, and ran a story on it. I'm not saying they're saints, but they are certainly both leaders whose values lean toward the altruistic.

Guided by these values, they had become increasingly uncomfortable with the company's strategy. It felt almost like a carrot and stick, and neither could see how Best Buy could build a future on a strategy that was fundamentally disrespectful to its customers.

From now on, they said, we will design our company to serve those customers who want to integrate our technology into their lives but who don't know how. We will serve the customer who is smart but confused by the products we sell, the customer who doesn't know whether he needs speakers with fifty watts per channel or two hundred, who isn't sure if he should buy an inkjet printer or a laser printer, who likes the look of our digital cameras but who doesn't understand what "resolution" means and can't figure out how to make prints. Yes, we will sell our products at the lowest price possible, but our emphasis will be less on price and more on learning what our customers want to learn and then teaching it to them. To this end, we will reduce the number of items we have on display. We will tear down these walls of televisions and cut our selection of VCRs from sixty to thirty-two. We will display only those products that we commit to keeping in stock, and we will train our salespeople to explain the relevant differences between each of these products. We will take our salespeople off commission and direct them toward helping rather than selling. In short, we will educate our customers and then allow these educated customers to make their own choices.

If all this sounds obvious, remember that Best Buy's competitors, with their emphasis on increased selection and increased commissions for salespeople, were ploughing ahead in the opposite direction. Of course hindsight now reveals that their instincts were right. Best Buy, redesigned to serve the customer who was smart but confused, grew powerful and strong. As Brad said in our interview, "The more we credited the customer's intelligence, and tried to increase it, the better we did."

This brings us up to 2003. Despite Best Buy's success, Brad decided that a further change was required. He's the kind of leader who views success as the art of leaping from one burning platform to the next and who, if he sees that the current platform isn't burning, will be more than pleased to set it on fire.

His insight was that the notion of serving the smart but confused customer, although clear, was still too broad. Brad, like any effective leader, spends more than 40 percent of his time in front of his customers, which in his case means in the stores. His frequent store visits brought home to him the fact that Best Buy actually had many masters. Different stores served very different customers with distinct needs. They were smart about different things and therefore confused about different things. If Best Buy was to take its commitment to serving the smart but confused customer to its logical conclusion, it would have to reinvent itself to accommodate each different type of customer.

To help him identify Best Buy's different masters, he brought together teams of smart people from around the company, and in conjunction with a Columbia finance professor, Larry Selden, they crunched through reams of customer purchase data and narrowed Best Buy's masters down to five. I am not at liberty to reveal all five, but I can tell you that one of them resembled the soccer mom who didn't care about having the newest and the best stuff—she just wanted a store that was easy to navigate with her kids and that showcased the few products that met her needs, so that she could find what she wanted quickly and get home. Another was the independent businessperson—the real estate agent, the general contractor, the insurance agent—who was most interested in what technology could do to help him manage his business more effectively.

Thus far, there was nothing particularly novel about what Brad was doing. Leaders have been segmenting their customers since Alfred Sloan, the legendary chief of General Motors, decided to offer a different brand of car—Chevrolet, Oldsmobile, Buick, Cadillac—for every level of income and lifestyle. What was novel, and in my estimation almost genius, was Brad's decision to focus each store on only one or two of these customer segments. This didn't reflect reality. The reality was that each store actually served a mix of each customer segment. But Brad decided to look past this reality and instead instructed each store to target only one or two of its many masters.

Part of the genius here is that Brad has brought intense clarity to each store. (The other part lies in the ripple effect, which I'll get to in a moment.) He has told the employees in each store who their primary audience is. He has shown them whom they are trying to please. In so doing, he has transformed their anxiety at having to please all of the people all of the time into confidence.

Visit Best Buy's Pasadena store, a store that is designed to serve primarily the soccer mom customer, and you discover what this confidence begets. The first thing you see is a car of painted plywood with two surfboards strapped to the roof. In the "seats" of this car are headrests, and in the headrests are small video screens playing the latest *Shrek* DVD. Next to the car are four or five computer playstations, set in brightly coloured display cases, a toddler play area enclosed by a red picket fence, and a row of shopping carts modified to look like race cars and fire engines.

None of these elements was designed and installed by Best Buy headquarters. Instead, each of them was the brainchild of one of the employees in the store. Charged with understanding and serving the soccer mom customer, the employees decided that the first thing she would want to see upon entering the store was a play area for her kids. So they built the wooden car one Saturday, painted it on Sunday, and, to add a little local colour, they decided to barter a flat screen television for a couple of surfboards from the surf shop down the street.

As one blue-shirted employee tells me, "We figured the kids would love to play in the car, but, at the same time, their mom would be interested to see how these video screens, which we sell, fit nicely into the seats' headrests. And, of course, if her kids enjoy watching the *Shrek* DVD, she can buy that here too."

He's excited, so he keeps going: "And do you see how we've done away with five-foot-high display shelving in this area? Mom won't feel comfortable if she can't see her kids, so we completely rearranged this area so that she has a clear line of sight from one end to the other. Sure, we lost some shelf space, but we knew she would appreciate it."

I visited another store in Westminster, California, and saw similar kinds of confident creativity. This store has been designed to serve the independent business owner, and the moment I enter the store I can see the impact of this focus. In a typical consumer electronics store similar products are displayed adjacent to one another—the full range of digital cameras are arrayed in the camera section, all the printers are stacked together in the printer section, and so on. But in this Best Buy store the products are jumbled up—a printer is displayed side by side with a digital camera, a global positioning system device stands next to a cell phone, with a laptop computer sandwiched in between. Looking closer, I realize that the products are not jumbled up so much as bundled together.

"Yes," says one of the blue-shirted clerks. "We decided that the independent business owner would want to see how all these different products could be linked together to make their job easier. This particular display you're looking at now is actually designed for an estate agent. Notice that we've bundled a laptop with a portable printer because they may want to download the specs of a particular house from the Web, print it out, and give it to their client right on the spot. We've also included a digital camera so that they can take pictures of the property and either e-mail them or print them out for their client. And then, of course, there's the GPS device, which is going to prevent them from getting lost as they drive around looking for a certain house."

"If I'm an estate agent, how do I know this bundle of products is designed for me?" I ask him.

"Well, we didn't want to ram it down their throats, but we figured if we could come up with a phrase that described their day-to-day life pretty well, then they'd be drawn over here to check out the bundle. So we made this sign." He points to a large cardboard sign that says, in quotes: "My office has four wheels."

I ask him if this bundling works, if it really drives sales, and he replies, "Not always. At first we didn't have the GPS device included in the bundle. We had a cell phone and a phone card instead. We thought this made sense, but for some reason no one was buying it. Then we came up with the idea of exchanging it for the GPS device. The folks back at corporate thought we were crazy. 'The GPS costs over thirteen hundred dollars,' they said. 'That's far more expensive than a phone. You won't sell any of them.' But we figured we'd try anyway. So we included the GPS and the whole bundle just took off. Now we can't keep the items in stock, we sell so many of them."

At that moment, almost as if it were scripted, a customer approaches us, looks up at the sign, down at the product bundle for maybe five minutes, and then decides to buy the entire display.

Then, as I am interviewing him to find out what he does and why he thought the $3,000 total purchase price was a good investment—he is a general contractor, as it turns out—another customer walks up, gives the products a cursory once-over, and then proceeds to do exactly the same.

This seemed almost too good to be real, so, later, I ask the store manager if this sort of thing happens all the time. He demurs. "No, I wish it did. But, I'll tell you, it happens often enough for us to be running 36 percent comps."

"Comps" is one of the most important metrics in retail. It refers to a store's comparative level of sales for the exact same day or week or month the previous year. If you are a retailer, one way to grow is to open many new stores. The problem with relying on this approach is that these new stores cost a lot to open and will deliver you only a short-lived sales spike. By far the best way to grow is to ensure that the stores that have been open for at least a year are selling more this year than they did over the same period last year. When this happens, you are said to have positive comps. If you can produce 10 percent positive comps, Wall Street is impressed. Twenty percent comps renders them speechless. Thirty-six percent comps, from an eight-year-old store like Westminster, which has had no significant refit or other capital investment, simply boggles their minds.

And the performance of the Westminster store isn't an exception. In store after store the discipline of trying to serve only one kind of customer has generated positive comps in the 25 to 35 percent range. Obviously, much of this increase in sales stems from the fact that the employees, guided by a clear focus on whom they are supposed to serve, are now more confident in their judgment, in their creativity, and in their initiative. In simple terms, they devise better ideas for how to present the store to the core customer.

Not all of these sales increases come from each store's core customer, however. A significant percentage must come from other types of customers who, although the store is not designed around their particular needs, nonetheless feel as though it is.

Brad's "ripple effect" explains this phenomenon. By challenging the employees in each store to focus on only one or two types of customers, Brad has cultivated their expertise in looking at the world through these customers' eyes. And so now, having practised and refined this expertise on these few customers, they know better how to apply it to all the others.

You see signs of this expertise everywhere. You see it in the home theatre section, where employees have printed up a sign reminding you that if you are thinking of buying a plasma television screen you should plan on adding an additional 20 percent for high-quality Monster cables—if you don't buy the cables you'll be wasting your money with a plasma screen, and we'd rather tell you this now than surprise you at the register. You can see it in the printer department, where someone has hooked up a bunch of different computers with a bunch of different printers so that, if you are so inclined, you can see for yourself the quality of each printer and each ink cartridge. You can see it in the computer department, where an employee has thought to move the register from against the back wall to right between the two shelves displaying the computers—most customers have questions while they are browsing the shelves, and now they can simply look over their shoulder and ask the blueshirt at the register. You can see it in the personal shopper programme—an innovation that was designed to help soccer moms find their way around the store, but that is now used, and loved, by all sorts of customers.

None of these changes are radical, some are commonsense, but, in combination and over time, they are powerful. They create in the customer the feeling that someone designed the store with their unique needs in mind.

No doubt every organization wants all of its many different kinds of customers to feel this way. Brad's insight is that the best way to achieve this is to focus your employees on only a few.

Surprisingly, when I ask Brad about the need for clarity, he questions it.

"I much prefer ambiguity to clarity," he says. "I think too much clarity leads to complacency. Instead, I want all of my people to feel free to challenge the accepted way of doing things and to experiment with new techniques. I think this is the only way to keep the organization curious and inquisitive. It's the only way to keep us alive."

But his questioning doesn't contradict the need for clarity about whom you are seeking to serve. As I've described, Brad is exceptionally vivid in showing employees whom their primary audience should be. What he is saying here is that a leader doesn't need to be clear on all points. Actually he is being more definitive than this. He is saying that a leader *must* not be clear on all points, and that one of the areas in which he should allow significant ambiguity is in the strategies and tactics selected by his employees. Yes, he should be clear about whom he is trying to serve, but then he must actively encourage his employees to devise novel and as yet unproven ways of serving them. As he says, this is the only way to keep the organization alive.

So, to excel as a leader, to transform anxiety into confidence, be clear about whom you are trying to serve. It is fine to commission research studies and focus groups if you are so inclined, but in the end your success will depend less on increasingly complex customer segmentation and more on your ability, once you've decided on your chosen customer, to describe the needs of this customer with great vividness. The confidence of your followers depends on this.

Thus far, the leaders we've quoted have all been very senior executives who have the authority to define for the entire organization whom it should seek to serve. Although, as we've seen, it is vital that they do this effectively, this doesn't imply that all other leaders in the organization should simply recite the chief executive's descriptions. Every division and every department within the organization exists to create something of value for a particular customer, either internal or external. If you find yourself leading one of these divisions or departments, it will be imperative that you define your group's customer as precisely and as vividly as, it is hoped, your CEO has done for the organization's customer. You might lead on a slightly smaller stage, but your followers' need for clarity about whom they are serving is just as acute.

And, of course, the same applies to the remaining three points of clarity.

## 2: What Is Our Core Strength?
Thirty years ago, in his book *The Effective Executive,* Peter

Drucker wrote that the most effective organizations "get their strengths together and make their weaknesses irrelevant." At the time this insight met with some scepticism. "Shouldn't an effective organization strive to be well-rounded? Isn't it only as strong as its weakest link?" These were sensible concerns, but, as happens with many Drucker insights, the intervening years have proven its accuracy.

Toyota has become the most successful automobile company in the world because it has chosen to make the most reliable cars in the world, not necessarily cars with the best performance or the most stylish designs.

Walgreens is the largest drugstore retailer in America (in terms of sales volume) not because it offers the cheapest products—most items can be bought more cheaply at stores such as Wal-Mart or Costco—but because it offers the most convenience. Most places you live, you're likely to find a Walgreens right around the corner, many of which will be open twenty-four hours, and which will be virtually guaranteed to have in stock the particular items you're looking for.

Microsoft has achieved world domination not through its design of end-user-friendly applications—many of its competitors offer applications that are more intuitive, more secure, and less likely to crash. Instead, it has built its empire almost entirely around its strength in partnering with large corporations. This partnering strength has enabled it to excel both at integrating its software with hardware manufacturers such as IBM, Dell, and Intel, and at selling this software/hardware package to Fortune 500 IT departments.

In direct contrast, Apple is rotten at partnering. It insists on controlling both the hardware and the software of its products, and it has never learned how to play nicely with corporate IT departments. Undoubtedly Apple has lost significant market share due to these weaknesses, but nonetheless Steve Jobs has been able to build a flourishing business by effectively leveraging its core strength, which he describes as "figuring out how to invent cool technology but making it wonderfully easy to use. That's what we have always done. That's what the Mac was." And that's what the iPods/iTunes combination is.

So, today, most smart observers agree that the strategy of "getting your strengths together and making your weaknesses irrelevant" is by far the most effective. What is less obvious is *why* it is such a powerful strategy. The most common explanation is the same one that is trotted out to explain why you need to be clear about whom you are trying to serve: namely that it helps you determine where you should be spending time and money and where you shouldn't. And as before, this asset allocation explanation has merit. Here's Jobs's further explanation, from an interview in 2004 with *The Wall Street Journal:*

> We look at a lot of things, but I'm as proud of the things that we have not done as I am of the ones we have done. . . . We got enormous pressure to do a PDA [personal digital assistant] and we looked at it and we said, Wait a minute, 90% of the people that use these things just want to get information out of them . . . and cellphones are going to do that. So getting into the PDA market means getting into the cellphone market. In the cell-

phone market you've got only five [companies to sell to]. And I just know we're not going to be very good at that.

On a more positive note, Walgreens, with its clear focus on convenience, decided to invest billions in its satellite-dependent - information system so that any Walgreens in the United States would be able to fill your prescription. Likewise, Toyota, with its emphasis on reliability, knows that time and money spent improving its manufacturing techniques will offer better returns than orienting itself around expensive, celebrity automobile designers like Chris Bangle at BMW and Michael Mauer at Porsche.

But, as before, despite the merits of this asset allocation explanation, it fails to get to the heart of the matter. The chief reason why it is so important for you, the leader, to be clear about the strength of your organization is more an emotional one than a rational one. We, your followers, are anxious about the future. To turn our anxiety into confidence, you must tell us why we will win. You must tell us why we will prevail in this better future you seem to see so clearly. There are many competitors out there. Why will we beat them? There are many obstacles in our path. Why will we overcome them? What advantages do we have? What is our edge? The more clearly you can answer these questions, the more confident we will be, and therefore the more resilient, and the more persistent, and the more creative.

Interestingly, the strengths you pick don't have to reflect present reality. You don't have to be right. You just have to be clear. Here I am not suggesting that you fudge the facts. I am simply telling you that your clarity is a constructive act. If you are clear, then we, your followers, will make you right.

These days, Brad Anderson is charging around the country telling everyone who will listen that the strength of Best Buy lies in the quality of its employees in the stores. "Our blueshirts," he says, "will be like the smartest friends you've ever had. We will be exceptionally careful about who we select for these roles. Those we select will be trained how to teach you what you want to learn. And we will arm them in the store with the best information technology possible so that they can answer any question you may have, even if it concerns a product that we don't sell."

Is he right that the strength of Best Buy lies in its blueshirts? I don't know. The last time you shopped in a Best Buy, you may or may not have had a fabulous experience. What's powerful about Brad's approach is not its present-day accuracy, but the impact it has on the future actions of all one hundred thousand of his employees. He is cutting through the complexity of their work and clarifying it for them. He is telling them that no matter what department they work in—marketing, merchandising, operations, inventory management, IT, human resources—they must orient their efforts toward ensuring that their colleagues in the stores are the best selected, the best trained, the best informed, and the best equipped in the business. And as such, he is giving them the confidence that comes from knowing if they can just do this one thing—strengthen the front line—Best Buy will win. This present-day confidence will create Best Buy's better future.

Of all the leaders I've studied, Preston Chiaro, president and chief executive of Rio Tinto Borax, the Rio Tinto subsidiary that mines and refines boron, offers the most compelling example of a leader who created a better reality by being clear, rather than necessarily accurate, about his organization's core strength.

On July 17, 1998, Rio Tinto, the mining multinational, suffered the most devastating accident in its history. In its talc mine in Lassing, Austria, a tunnel collapsed, trapping a miner, Georg Hainzl. A squad of ten workers was assembled and sent down into the mine to attempt a rescue. As they descended into the main shaft, a second mud slide burst through the retaining walls, killing all ten. Ten days later, a miracle. Georg Hainzl was discovered eking out an existence in a waterlogged air pocket and was lifted to safety.

Six months after this tragedy, Preston was named president of Borax. Motivated perhaps by the Lassing tragedy, perhaps by his previous experience as an environmental engineer, he decreed that from this point on Borax's strength would be its safety record. "There is simply no reason," he announced, "why every employee should not be as healthy when they leave the mine in the evening as they were when they reported for work in the morning. We at Borax will be the safest mining operation in all of Rio Tinto, and we will bet that if we are, then everything else—productivity, efficiency, profitability—will take care of itself."

This statement didn't reflect current reality—the year Preston took the reins, Borax experienced thirty-eight total injuries and twenty-six lost-time injuries, a performance that put them squarely in the middle of the Rio Tinto pack of companies. But it was vivid. It was clear. And this clarity galvanized every single employee to make it come true. Today, when you visit one of

their facilities you soon become aware that this one claim—
"our strength is our safety"—informs every action, every
process, every meeting. In fact, in all of my research, I can't
think of a company that is so dominated by one ideal.

Driving up to Borax's mine in the town of Boron (creative
town-naming is clearly not a strength) a few miles north of
Edwards Air Force Base in California's high desert, the first
thing that greets me is a large roadside sign proclaiming their
safety mission:

> *Borax protects and promotes the health and safety of
> everyone who works at or visits our facilities. Our ulti-
> mate goal is to prevent all injuries and illness through-
> out our global operations.*

Intrigued, but not yet impressed—mission statements are
like campaign promises: easy to make, hard to live up to—I
pause to scribble it down and then drive on. And immediately
I come upon a sign that somehow measures my speed and spits
it back out to me on a large digital display: 38, 39, 38, 41.

"SLOW DOWN," it shouts at me. "THE SPEED LIMIT IS
25 MPH."

I look around guiltily and ease the car down to twenty-five.

At the gate, the attendant asks my business, makes a call to
confirm my appointment, and then leans forward to say, "Listen. I am about to give you a Safety Training Certificate. Before
I do, I have to ask you a few questions. Will you commit to ob-
serving the speed limit while driving within the facility?"

"Er, yes," I reply, feeling even guiltier now.

"Will you wear your seat belt at all times?"

"Yes."

"And will you wear this"—she hands me a hard hat—"when you enter the mine?"

"Yes, I will."

Suitably chastened, I drive to the administration building, passing another large sign that reads, "The Boron Mine: 821,427 hours without a lost-time accident," park the car, and am then escorted to my meeting room. Three Borax executives file in, pleasantries are exchanged, and then I launch into one of my prepared questions.

"Look," interrupts one, "before we start, Marcus, I should tell you that the winds can get pretty strong up here, particularly on Highway 58. So, when you're driving home, make sure you keep both hands on the wheel."

"Er, thanks."

"Yes," says another. "I've found that the winds are not only strong but gusty. Don't let a period of relative calm fool you into letting go with those hands. Around the next corner the wind is going to blow like crazy."

"While we're at it," chimes in the first one, "you need to know that there are three alarms that you might hear in this building. One is a loud beeping. This signals that everyone should evacuate the building. The second is a continuous blaring noise. This signals that everyone should congregate in the atrium. And the third is an intruder alarm. It sounds like this." He makes a strange whooping sound. "If you hear this one, just stay put in this meeting room." He goes on to tell me where the exit routes are, to point out the emergency phone numbers on my Safety Training Certificate, and to show me the safest way to lift up my heavy shoulder bag.

This is all well and good, but it's taking up a lot of time. So, just as he is about to launch into a warning about the sonic booms from the jet fighters overhead, I interject, "I don't mean to be rude, but I am not here to talk about safety. Don't think I don't appreciate your concern—I do. But can we press on with my questions now, please?"

They pause, embarrassed; embarrassed for me. What I have been witnessing, I learn, isn't some show put on to impress an inquisitive visitor. It is a routine event at Borax.

When Preston became president he decided that every meeting should begin with a five-minute discussion on safety, a "safety share", he called it. It didn't matter what the meeting was supposed to be about. And it didn't matter if the safety advice concerned personal safety rather than work safety. Every meeting must begin with a safety share.

This discipline was but one small component of Preston's overarching commitment to making safety Borax's strength. In his view, Borax would not become strong at safety simply by improving the working conditions. Yes, he said, we need to ensure that all work spaces are well lit, that steps and stair rails are well maintained, and that equipment is safely stored, but these physical improvements are not enough. To make safety a strength we must dramatically change the attitude of every single employee. We must make safety everyone's priority. We must seed safety everywhere.

During the course of two days spent at two different sites, I came to appreciate just how successfully he has achieved this.

For example, every employee must complete a Personal Safety Improvement Plan. The mine manager, John Kinneberg, includes on his list not only work items, such as:

- I will introduce the equipment simulator to drive down equipment damage accidents.

But also personal safety to-dos:

- I will undergo a screening for skin cancer, and will always wear sunscreen.
- I will drive to the conditions, drive defensively, and will drive to the "5 Keys" that I learned in the Smith driving course.

And even:

- I will spend time with my children to stress the importance of working safely in the yard and in the home.

Every employee has been trained on the five safety behaviours, and when I quiz employees at random during my visits, all seem able to recite them instantaneously:

- Keep your eyes on your path.
- Keep your eyes on your hands.
- Be aware of the line of fire.
- Always anticipate letting go.

- When working on a piece of equipment, isolate and de-energize it.

A new award has been created to honour the mine's twenty safest employees. These twenty Safety Mules—so called because of the twenty-mule teams that, back in the 1920s, were used to haul the boron ore out of the desert (after which their 20 Mule Team Borax was also named)—combine for a total of 711 years without an injury. Gene Van Horn is the lead safety mule. He has worked at Borax as a shipping clerk for fifty-three years and has never been injured on the job.

Borax's commitment to safety is now so ingrained that it extends to include even the safety of the animal life surrounding the mine. For example, Borax now employs a professional turtle handler. The California desert turtle lives in close proximity to the mine in Boron, and occasionally he is surprised by miners and engineers going about their work. When surprised in this way, the turtle's unfortunate reflex is to empty his bladder on the spot. The desert turtle has many qualities, but speed isn't one of them, and so, stranded far from a much-needed supply of water, more often than not he succumbs to dehydration. The turtle handler's job is to sneak up on him from behind and tuck his tail under his legs to prevent him from urinating, or if he or she is too late to stop this, to scoop him up and carry him carefully to a nearby puddle or creek.

If this last example appears absurd, a bizarre exercise in public relations for the mine, Preston is unconcerned. He lets his company's performance speak for itself. In 1999, Borax employees suffered thirty-eight total injuries. Today this number has fallen to thirteen. The improvement in serious injuries, measured as lost-time injuries, is even more impressive. In 1999 there were twenty-six. In 2003, there were four; a performance that earned Borax the Chief Executive's Safety Award. And, as Preston predicted, other performance metrics have risen accordingly. Today, Rio Tinto Borax is more productive, more efficient, and, as measured by return to shareholders, more valuable than at any time in its history.

Of course, there may be many factors causing Borax to excel on these last three metrics, but Preston is convinced that his "our strength is our safety" initiative is one of them. Having looked closely at his operation, sceptically at first and then with increasing admiration, I am inclined to agree with him.

At any rate, it is hard not to be impressed with the self-assurance of employees who, having suffered a crisis of confidence after the Lassing disaster, now believe unreservedly that they will win because they are safe.

If you want your people to follow you confidently into a better future, take a leaf out of Preston's book. Tell them clearly where their core strength lies, and, thus focused, thus fortified, they will do everything in their power to make it come true.

### 3: What Is Our Core Score?

During the research for this book I interviewed General Sir David Ramsbotham. Having reached the rank of adjutant general of the British army, Sir David retired and soon after was appointed chief inspector of Her Majesty's prisons. When he took over, the British prison system was in a terrible state. Today, under the scourge of his leadership, significant improvements have been made, although he would be the first to admit that much remains to be done.

What did you do? I asked him straight away. How did you bring about change?

"To tell you the truth, there was a limit to what I could do. I was the chief inspector, you see, and as such I couldn't actually go in and tell the heads of the prisons to change their ways. Instead I had to make things happen by altering the way that we inspected the prisons, which, in the end, meant altering the way we measured the success of a prison. As I look back, finding a better way to measure success was probably my most important contribution."

"How did Britain measure the success of its prisons?" I asked.

"We used to rely on one key metric: number of escapees."

I smiled.

"It's not as silly as it appears, Marcus," he said. "How many people did you manage to keep in it? is actually quite a sensible question to ask of a prison."

"So why did you reject it as the core score?"

"Well, I began by thinking about who exactly a prison is designed to serve. And, on reflection, I decided that the main purpose of a prison system is not to serve society by keeping prisoners off the streets. This is certainly one of its purposes, but not its main purpose. The main purpose of a prison should be to serve the prisoner. By which I mean that we must do something to the prisoner while he is in prison so that when he is released back into society he is less likely to commit another crime. Not everyone agreed with this conclusion, Marcus, but since I was convinced it was right, there was really only one possible score we should use to measure the success of a prison: number of repeat offenders."

In hindsight, it may seem obvious to you that number of repeat offenders, or recidivism rate as it's sometimes called, is by far the best way to measure the long-term success of a prison system. But most keen insights appear obvious in hindsight. The trick is to see them as obvious in advance and then act on them, which Sir David proceeded to do, with all the discipline and focus that you would expect of an ex-army man.

Armed with his new score, he turned the prison world upside-down—prisons viewed as successful under the old scoring system were relegated to the bottom, and vice versa. He challenged the management teams of each prison to alter their focus and to devote their energies toward figuring out new programmes to rehabilitate the prisoners while they were incarcerated and better ways to ease them back into society once they were released. As you would expect, progress varied according to the quality of each prison's management team, but everyone involved in Britain's prison system was forced to reexamine their priorities and their achievements.

My purpose in recounting Sir David's experiences is not to delve into the complexities of prison reform—they are many, and deserve books of their own. Rather, my purpose is first to remind you of the power of scores. The old truisms tell us that "what gets measured gets managed" and "you get what you inspect", and they survive as truisms because they are manifestly true.

And second, to suggest that it is your responsibility as a leader to sort through all the many things that can be measured and identify the one score that we, your followers, should focus on. If you want us to follow you, you must tell us what score we should use to measure our progress into the forest of the future. This forest is dark and deep, and therefore unnerving, and so you must tell us the core score that will reveal how far we have all come, and how far we have yet to go.

Don't give us a scorecard with five or ten or twenty metrics on it. Don't take all the many metrics that our organization can generate and present them to us as your "balanced scorecard". Balancing your scorecard might make you, the analytical leader, happy, because now you have succeeded in imposing some order on your complex world. But we, your followers, don't really care how balanced your scorecard is. It may be balanced, or it may not. Either way, it is still too complex. It contains too many scores. And as such it tells us that we should look here, and here, and here, and here to gauge our journey. This complexity confuses us and makes us anxious. It saps our strength and undermines our confidence.

If you still want to design a balanced scorecard, keep it to yourself and your fellow executives. Pull it out at board meetings. Refer to it at executive retreats. Use it on the performance scorecards of your direct reports if you wish. But don't broadcast it to us. Don't make it the cornerstone of your efforts at leadership. If you want us to follow you into the future, you must cut through its complexity and give us one metric, one number to track our progress. Give us a score that we can do something about, or that measures how well we are serving the people you have told us we should be serving, or that quantifies the strength you have assured us we possess. If you can identify the core score that can do some or all of these things, we will reward you with our confidence.

This is what Preston Chiaro did. As it turns out, Preston is quite a fan of balanced scorecards and requires all his direct reports to draw one up for themselves. He even insists that they post these scorecards on the company's intranet so that any employee can inspect them. But he realizes that a balanced scorecard is a device to help him manage, not lead. It will help him set expectations for one person, but it will not help him bring clarity to many people. Only something like his "our strength is our safety" initiative can do this, and so this is why he focuses on, publicizes, and celebrates one core score: number of lost-time injuries.

This is also what Brad Anderson did. Having told his people whom they should be serving, and that their strength lay in the intelligence, insight, and creativity of the front-line employees, he then went the required next step and identified the one score that would track their progress toward a better future: number of engaged employees.

Best Buy uses twelve simple questions to measure employee engagement. These include such questions as "Do you know what is expected of you at work?"; "At work does someone seem to care about you?"; and "At work do you have an opportunity to do what you do best every day?" (You can find all twelve, labelled the Q12 by Gallup researchers, in the first chapter of my book *First, Break All the Rules.*) Although Best Buy generates a multitude of daily performance scores—sales, profit, shrink, accessories, warranties, to name a few of the more obvious ones—Brad decided that the most important score was how many employees in each store felt fully engaged at work. He reasoned that customers would be well served, and that the front line would be intelligent, insightful, and creative, only insofar as each employee was being managed superbly. In essence, this meant clear expectations, roles that fit their talents, managers who cared about them and praised them when they excelled, a sense that they were always learning and growing at work—in short, the conditions measured by the twelve-question survey.

Although Best Buy's success could be measured in a variety of different ways, Brad's bet was that if each store could increase the number of its engaged employees it would subsequently see an increase in the more traditional measures of corporate success. The numbers have borne him out. Today he can point to data that show that across the entire Best Buy enterprise an increase in employee engagement of 2 percent (as measured by the twelve employee survey questions) results in an additional $70 million in profitability.

Mayor Rudy Giuliani made a similar bet. Although he could have targeted many possible scores to measure the success of New York City, Giuliani, like all effective leaders, recognized the power of focusing his people on only one. He chose crime statistics, and in doing so, he wasn't ignoring all the other scores. He was simply betting that if he and his team could reduce crime, then every other score—the city's credit rating, the number of tourism visits, the number of new businesses opened, and even the number of successful child adoptions—would rise.

The data confirm the wisdom of his bet. During his eight-year tenure, crime, as you would have predicted given his focus on it, plummeted—overall crime down by 57 percent, murder down by two-thirds, 1,200 fewer rapes, 62,000 fewer burglaries. What some might not have predicted was the improvement in all the other scores. From 1994 to 2001, successful adoptions increased from 1,784 to 3,148; 200 new businesses opened in Harlem alone; tourist visits increased from 25.8 million to 37.4 million; and the debt rating service, Moody's, upped the city's credit rating from Baa1 to A2.

In highlighting the achievements of these leaders, my point is not that each of them picked the one "right" score. There is no "right" score. In contrast to Giuliani, consider Ken Livingstone, the current mayor of London, who has chosen to focus the city on reducing not crime, but traffic congestion, and has risked his popularity to pursue this focus. It will now cost you five pounds to drive your car into the centre of London.

My point here is that by zeroing in on one core score these leaders brought clarity to their people. This clarity made people more confident, more persistent, more resilient, and more creative, and these qualities then spilled over, or "rippled" to use Brad Anderson's word, into all areas of the enterprise.

If you want to match their achievements, you should do the same. Sort through all the scores available and pick one that fits whom your people are trying to serve, or that quantifies the strength you say they possess, and, most important, that they can do something to affect. And having picked it, broadcast it, publicize it, and celebrate it. Announce to your people that if they want to know how far they've come in their journey toward a better future, this is the one core score in which they should place their faith.

Ideally this score will be a leading indicator of success, such as employee engagement or employee safety or crime, rather than a trailing indicator, such as sales or profit or tax revenues, but, from the perspective of your followers, what matters most is that it's clear.

### 4: What Actions Can We Take Today?

Telling a leader to take action is almost as beside the point as urging a basketball player to take a shot. Like the basketball player, the leader has many responsibilities while on the "court," but unless these activities lead to a moment when he pulls up, aims at his target, and shoots, then nothing good will happen. And like the basketball player, the leader knows that, although many shots will miss their target, he must keep shooting nonetheless. Every shot, hit or miss, will teach him something about himself, his situation, his team, and his competitors, all of which should lead to a better, more focused shot the next time around. And besides, in the words of basketball great Wayne Gretzky (all right, maybe he played a little hockey, too), the effective leader knows he'll miss 100 percent of shots he never takes.

So, yes, the leader must take action because only action leads to impact. But actions also possess a separate, equally powerful quality. Actions are unambiguous. They are clear. If you, the leader, can highlight a few carefully selected actions, then we, your followers, will happily latch on to these actions and use them to calm our fear of the unknown. Guided by the clarity of your action, we will no longer have to infer the future from such theoretical pronouncements as your "core values" or your "mission statement". We will simply look to see what actions you are taking and found our faith and our confidence on these.

If you are going to use actions in this way—as clarifiers, rather than simply instruments of change—be aware that we will respond best to two distinct types of action: systematic action and symbolic action. Each is powerful, but each clarifies in a different way.

Systematic action interrupts our day-to-day routines and forces us to become involved in new activities. It disrupts us.

Symbolic action doesn't alter what we do; it just grabs our attention. It distracts us, thereby giving us something new and vivid on which to focus.

The effective leader knows how to use both to great effect.

When Rudy Giuliani assumed the leadership of New York City, yes, he talked concepts. He announced his desire to improve the quality of life, to reduce crime, to stimulate business, and so return the city to what he perceived to be its former glory. But he also deliberately drew our attention to three actions that he would take immediately. First, he would remove the squeegee men. For as long as most New Yorkers could remember, the squeegee men were a fixture of life in the city. They would position themselves amongst the lines of cars waiting to enter or exit Manhattan through the bridges and the tunnels and would earn a living by throwing a dirty, wet rag over your windshield and demanding payment to clean the mess up. Giuliani decided that this was a terrible first and last impression of the city, so he vowed to eradicate the problem. Whatever New Yorkers may have thought of the legal strategy he employed—he had the squeegee men arrested for jaywalking—what they appreciated was that in under a month they were gone.

Second, Giuliani decreed that he would get rid of all the graffiti on the city's buses and subway cars. This proved to be quite a challenge—technically, the Transit Authority is responsible for these vehicles, not the city itself—but by pulling together representatives from twenty different agencies he was able to cut through the bureaucratic fog and get it done.

And third, he altered the taxi and limousine regulations to state that, henceforth, every cabdriver would be required to wear a collared shirt. In his view, it reflected badly on the city that the first thing a visitor would see upon arrival at an airport or a train station was a scruffy cabdriver in a sweaty white T-shirt.

I don't know if these actions were the right ones to take, but, as someone living in New York at the time, I do know that each of them was powerfully symbolic. Not only did they reveal that Giuliani was a leader who could get things done, but, more important, they grabbed our attention and showed us vividly the kind of better future he was trying to create.

While the ridding of the squeegee men, the subway graffiti, and the collarless cabdrivers were symbolic actions, the Comp-Stat initiative was systematic. Early in his administration he was told by a deputy police commissioner, Jack Maple, that New York City had the ability to measure and report crime statistics on a daily basis. This was a major advantage over most cities, who were still relying on the FBI's quarterly or even yearly reports on the seven major crime categories—murder, rape, robbery, felonious assault, burglary, grand larceny, and grand larceny auto. These data were useful for gauging trends, but, because they lagged so far behind the present, they were almost useless at guiding action.

Armed with daily crime data, Giuliani disrupted the regular police department schedule by instituting a twice-weekly CompStat meeting. At this new CompStat meeting, held at 7:00 a.m. every Thursday and Friday at One Police Plaza, more than one hundred senior police officers would gather together to discuss the patterns in the data. At each meeting a commander from one of New York City's eight borough commands would have to stand up in front of his peers and both explain and defend what was going on within his borough. These could be tough meetings, as Giuliani describes: "In those days, the colourful, bow-tied Jack Maple would pepper the precinct commander with 'Why are car thefts down 20 percent citywide, but up 10 percent in your area?' Or: 'Explain how assaults have been falling for six straight months until last month, then started rising?' " However, he believed that these tough meetings were necessary because, in his words, "They encouraged transparency, accountability, holistic analysis, and the sharing of best practices."

The mayor was right about these outcomes, however each of them was actually a *management* outcome. These outcomes didn't give people confidence in a better future. Instead, what they did was show each individual what the mayor's expectations were and what the individual could do to meet these expectations.

The true *leadership* power of these meetings lay in their

clarity. They forced people to change their comfortable routines and engage in unambiguously new behaviours. In essence, what Giuliani was telling his people was, "I don't care where you used to be at 7:00 a.m. on Thursdays and Fridays, but from this point on, you will be at my CompStat meeting. When I talk about building a better future for New York City, this meeting, and all that happens here, is precisely what I mean." While few of the participants would have enjoyed being publicly grilled by his boss, in the end, all of them, whether consciously or not, will have drawn strength from this level of clarity.

On close investigation, you will find that virtually every effective leader excels at using both symbolic and systematic action. At Borax, Preston Chiaro's setting up of signs broadcasting his company's safety mission, safety record, and even a visitor's speed limit were all symbolic actions, as were the practices of giving all visitors a Safety Training Certificate, of rewarding the twenty Safety Mules, and even of employing a turtle handler. In contrast, the discipline of the "safety share" and the Personal Safety Improvement Plan were systematic actions. They made new behaviours routine.

When Brad Anderson decided to move the computer help desk from the far back of the store ("Why would we publicize the fact that our computers might break down?") to the very front of the store ("We know they break down. And when they do, we are here to help you.") this symbolized that the new Best Buy would respect the intelligence and the needs of its customers. Whereas when he decreed that all stores would be judged on how engaged their employees were, and that routines would be altered to allow time to administer the employee engagement survey, review the results, and decide how to improve them, these were disruptive, systematic actions.

Or think back to the mining crew boss, Randy Fogle. When he told his men to pull the tarpaulin across the entrance of their little cave, this was a symbolic action—it distracted them from the rising waters and allowed their minds to focus on something more hopeful. Moe's rescue was also a symbolic action—not for Moe, obviously, but for the others. The rescue of their comrade rallied their spirits and gave them hope that they, too, would be rescued. But, as with all effective leaders, Randy knew that symbolism, although powerful, would not suffice. He needed to jolt his men out of their despair and give them something systematic to do, something that would make their better future more vivid and real. Hence his idea to set up a routine whereby, every hour, two miners would wade down through the tunnel to the spot where the rescuers had broken through the mine roof and then hammer three times on the exposed drill bit to remind those on the surface that this was a rescue, not a recovery.

So, as you strive to lead us toward a better future, remember that we need clarity, and that actions, both the symbolic and the systematic, can be wonderfully, comfortingly clear. If you can sort through all the actions available to you and identify the few that can either grab our attention or alter our routines, then our confidence in you and your better future will grow strong.

## THE DISCIPLINES OF LEADERSHIP

*"How do the best leaders achieve this clarity?"*

In conversation with an executive the other day, I was busy emphasizing his followers' need for clarity when he brought me up short with this question: If clarity is so vital to effective leadership, how do I achieve it?

It was a fair question. Most executives have calendars that are chockablock with meetings and commitments. In fact, during the course of my research for this book, the difficulty I experienced in arranging time with exemplary leaders reminded me of the famous *New Yorker* cartoon where an executive, having scanned the calendar on his desk, says cheerfully into the phone, "How about never? Is never good for you?"

And the challenge for the busy leader is not simply that she has meetings back to back, but also that each of these meetings requires an entirely different focus. Today's leader is expected to have the mental agility to leap from a succession planning discussion, to an appearance on CNBC, to a decision about whether or not to fire the advertising agency, to a real estate transaction, and back to the succession planning discussion.

So, faced with this barrage of diverse demands, what can you do to find the clarity your followers require?

There are several steps you can take, limited only by one fundamental recognition: your ability to distill from your complex world a clear insight into whom your organization is trying to serve, or what its core strength is, or what score you should target, or what symbolic and systematic actions you should highlight is partly determined by your talents.

For those whose minds so delight in ambiguity and subtlety that they can't bear to land on anything definitive, no amount of skills training will make them comfortable leaving an avenue of investigation unexplored or a door of possibility unopened. Over time they may come to be appreciated for their creativity, but they will never be known for their clarity. There are important and rewarding roles for such people, roles that require, above all things, open-ended-possibility thinking, but leadership isn't one of them.

But more than likely, if you aspire to leadership, you do indeed possess some talent for distillation, for piercing complexity and finding clarity. And, if you do, the question then becomes "What can you do to refine this talent, and so prepare yourself for leadership roles of increasing depth and breadth?"

From my research it is apparent that, although no two leaders are identical, all effective leaders do seem to develop in their working lives certain disciplines that aid them in their quest for clarity. Let me close this chapter with a brief description of the three most prevalent disciplines. Any one of these disciplines, when practiced with rigour, will help you increase your effectiveness as a leader.

### Discipline 1: Take Time to Reflect.

First, the best leaders I've studied all discipline themselves to take time out of their working lives to think. They all muse. They all reflect. They all seem to realize that this thinking time is incredibly valuable time, for it forces them to process all that has happened, to sift through the clutter, to run ideas up the proverbial flagpole and then yank them down again, and, in the end, to conclude. It is this ability to draw conclusions that allows them to project such clarity.

Brad Anderson disciplines himself to take a two-hour walk every week. Yes, this helps to keep him fit, but it also gives him time to ruminate.

Sir Terry Leahy refuses to carry a cell phone. He has identified his time in cars, trains, and planes as his most productive thinking time and he guards it jealously. Besides, he says, people know where I'm going. They can reach me when I get there.

Dan Cathy, the president of Chick-fil-A, disciplines himself to go into seclusion in his cabin in the hills of North Georgia once a quarter. When I asked him what he does during this day, he replied, "Nothing. I just use it as a time to remind myself of those few things that I am certain of."

And what do effective leaders think about during this musing time? All manner of things, I imagine, but the list of topics always includes excellence. They all think about success. Why is this operation doing so much better than the others? Why are these customers so much more loyal than the rest? Why is this management team so much more resilient and persistent than my other teams? Unlike most social scientists, they understand that success is not the opposite of failure. It is simply different, and therefore, if they are to pick out its distinct characteristics, it demands their focus. In essence, they realize that the only thing more damaging than not understanding why something failed is failing to understand why something succeeded. After all, if they can't parse success, they will be hard-pressed to repeat it.

Since by now you are quite familiar with Brad Anderson's situation, I'll give you an example from his world. He began his customer-centricity initiative in 2004 with a pilot programme of thirty stores located in various parts of the country. Each store was told which customer segment it should focus on, and then the employees in each store were educated about the needs of their particular segment and given suggestions devised by corporate, such as the personal shopper programme or the bundling of products to reflect the customer's lifestyle, for how to meet these needs.

Although all of the stores improved their performance, Brad quickly saw that eight of the pilot stores were dramatically outperforming the rest, achieving positive comps in the mid-thirties. This variation in performance worried him. Why were these eight stores doing so much better? What key ingredient did they have that the others lacked? If he couldn't identify it, he wouldn't be able to replicate it, and if he couldn't replicate it he wouldn't be confident in rolling out his customer-centricity initiative across the entire enterprise.

So he visited the eight stores, talked with the customers, watched the employees, and then visited the other stores and talked with their customers and employees, and then went back to the eight exemplary stores and talked and listened and watched some more. And each week he took his walk, and he thought about it all.

And after a couple of months he reached his conclusion. The eight stores were not excelling because they were newer, or because they were all focusing on the same customer segment, or because they were all in urban rather than mall locations. They were excelling because their employees were more engaged. They were more spirited, more confident, and, in the end, a great deal more creative at figuring out how to meet their customer's needs.

For example, across all thirty stores, 14 percent of customers were taking advantage of the personal shopper programme. Among the eight best, this number reached as high as 50 percent. Why? Simply because a few employees, having deduced that customers were too nervous to march in and request a personal shopper, invented a new role, called the entertainment specialist, whose chief responsibility was to get to know the customers while they were browsing (usually in the CD and DVD aisles, hence the name entertainment specialist), to explain the concept of the personal shopper, and then, if necessary, walk the customers over and introduce them to the personal shopper himself.

The ideas for bartering the flat screen television for the surfboards, and for building the plywood car, and for designing the children's play area, and for substituting the expensive GPS device for the cell phone in the "My office has four wheels" bundle were all generated by employees in the eight top performing stores.

Brad concluded that these ideas were not the product of more talented employees. They were the product of employees who had been encouraged to find ways to connect their talents to the needs of their customers. In short, he concluded that these employees, beginning with the vice presidents and extending through all departments and levels, were simply better managed.

This didn't seem to him, and probably doesn't to you, like a genius-level epiphany. It was simply a conclusion. But having arrived at it, he had confidence in it. It clarified things for him. And this clarity then informed all his subsequent decisions, one of which, you will recall, was his decision to use "number of engaged employees" as Best Buy's core score for tracking its progress into the future.

### Discipline 2: Select Your Heroes with Great Care.

The second discipline of effective leaders is the care with which they select their heroes. And here I'm not referring to their role models—although many good leaders are indeed able to tell you explicitly whom they admire. Instead, I'm referring to those employees whose performance they choose to celebrate. If you want to predict the future behaviour of any community of people—a team, a tribe, a company, even a country—look to its heroes. Look to the people and the events it chooses to revere.

For example, if you want to predict the behaviour of my fellow Britons, hang out for a while in a history class or dip into a couple of our history textbooks. Pretty soon you will discover that we are particularly proud of three events: the Charge of the Light Brigade during the Crimean War and, from World War II, the evacuation of Dunkirk and the Battle of Britain. On the surface, there's nothing remarkable about this. Most countries elevate a few carefully selected military exploits to almost mythical status: the Russians have their Stalingrad; the U.S. has Washington crossing the Delaware and the Omaha Beach land-ings; the Islamic world has Saladin's liberation of Jerusalem in the twelfth century.

However, investigate Britain's three battles and you'll notice something distinctly odd: we didn't win any of them. We lost two, while the third, the Battle of Britain, could generously be declared a tie.

So, if we didn't win them, why do we celebrate them? Simply because they capture perfectly what we consider to be our core strength: the willingness to persevere when our backs are against the wall. This is why we revere Winston Churchill and his claim, "We will fight them on the beaches. . . . We will never surrender." We British may not win, but you can rest assured that, no matter what the odds, we will never give up. We are the Avis of nations: we try harder.

You can even hear it in our national song, "Rule, Britannia", the chorus of which announces:

*Rule, Britannia! Britannia rules the waves,*
*Britons never, never, never shall be slaves.*

"We shall never be slaves" isn't really much of a claim, is it. But there it is, right at the core of our national character. Perseverance and effort are everything. Winning is a distant third.

No one better embodies the British sporting motto of "it's not the winning but the taking part that counts" than Eddie "The Eagle" Edwards. To any other nation Edwards would be a strange sporting hero indeed, but that is exactly what he became to the British public at the 1988 Winter Olympics in Calgary, where he managed to come dead last in his chosen sport of Ski-jumping. It was his perseverance in the face of adversity and his willingness to try that won him a place in our hearts. So what if he came fifty-eighth out of fifty-eight skiers at the Games, at least he'd given it a good shot.

Contrast this with the United States. The U.S. is the most competitive of nations, a nation where, in Vince Lombardi's words, "Winning isn't everything. It's the only thing." The proof for this can be found on the sports pages of any newspaper. In the U.K., the sports pages are filled with tales of derring-do and heroic effort, which usually wind up in performances just the wrong side of victory. In the U.S., the stories are overwhelmed by the numbers, column upon column of batting averages, RBIs, yards gained, points scored, assists made, and winning percentages. In fact, if you don't look closely, it's easy to confuse the sports section with the business section.

Why this preoccupation with scores? Because competitors love scores. If you can measure it, you can compare it, and if you can compare, you can compete, and if you can compete, you can win. America's core strength is not trying, but winning—look, here are the heroes and their scores to prove it.

National differences aside, bear in mind that, as a leader, you must remember that the employees you choose to celebrate will reveal the future you are trying to create. When you bring an employee up onstage and praise her performance, this has a management impact. It will make this particular employee feel appreciated and will motivate her to do even better. However, it will also, if you do it well, have a leadership impact. If you can tell us, your followers, exactly what she did to deserve this recognition, if you can show us the people she served, or the strength she embodied, or the scores she achieved, or the actions she took, you will make everything much clearer. You are pointing to her and telling us that, although she is by no means perfect, her specific behaviours are the building blocks of our better future.

In short, the heroes you select will serve to clarify our future.

### Discipline 3: Practise.

The final discipline employed by the best leaders is this: they practise. They discipline themselves to practise the words, the images, and the stories they will use to help us perceive the future more clearly.

Do you think Doug Degn just came up with "People who live paycheque to paycheque" on the spur of the moment? I don't. I think he practised it. I think he tried out a variety of different word combinations in e-mails, hallway conversations, meetings, and presentations, and landed on the "paycheque to paycheque" line because this was the particular word combination that seemed to resonate most strongly with his audiences.

The most effective leaders don't waste time trying to come up with newer and better speeches. Instead, having practised and refined their speech, they seek out new and bigger audiences and then give the same speech.

Dr. Martin Luther King Jr. offers us the best example of this. Most of us know excerpts of his "I have a dream" speech so well that we can recite them by heart. What some may not know is that, for the two million marchers for jobs and freedom, he had been persuaded by the leadership of the NAACP and the Southern Christian Leadership Conference to prepare a very different speech from the one we all know. This is a huge platform, they told him, a unique opportunity, and so it requires a new speech, different from the one you have been accustomed to giving. He stayed up half the night writing and rewriting this new speech, which began with a metaphor likening the U.S. Constitution to a promissory note, written by the Founding Fathers, which the current generation of disenfranchised African-Americans was now poised to cash.

It was a good metaphor, but eight minutes into the speech he realized that it wasn't hitting home. He was losing his audience. And since two million people is a lot to lose, he did what all effective leaders would have done. He ditched the new speech he had been coerced into writing and reverted back to the words, the images, and the phrasings that he had used time and time again in churches and meeting halls. The excerpts of the speech that most of us can recite, such as "I have a dream that my four little children will one day live in a nation where they will not be judged by the colour of their skin, but by the content of their character," are images that Dr. King resorted to because he knew that they would work. They had worked before, and on that hot afternoon in the summer of 1963, he had confidence that they would work again.

I am not suggesting that you strive to achieve the same rhetorical prowess as Dr. King. He was blessed with a talent for oratory that few of us will ever possess. But you can learn from his lesson. Discipline yourself to practise your descriptions of the future. Experiment with word combinations. Discard the ones that fall flat and keep returning again and again to the ones that seem to resonate and provide us with the clarity we seek.

And, above all, do not worry about being repetitious. Just when you are starting to get bored by the sound of your own voice may well be the very moment when you finally reach into our minds, pierce our confusion, and allow us to see for the first time your, and our, better future.

•  •  •

Effective leaders don't have to be passionate. They don't have to be charming. They don't have to be brilliant. They don't have to possess the common touch. They don't have to be great speakers. What they must be is clear. Above all else, they must never forget the truth that of all the human universals—our need for security, for community, for clarity, for authority, and for respect—our need for clarity, when met, is the most likely to engender in us confidence, persistence, resilience, and creativity.

Show us clearly whom we should seek to serve, show us where our core strength lies, show us which score we should focus on and which actions must be taken today, and we will reward you by working our hearts out to make our better future come true.

## PART II

# The One Thing
# You Need to Know

## *SUSTAINED INDIVIDUAL SUCCESS*

CHAPTER 5

# The Twenty Percenters

Half an hour into a long flight from Orlando to Los Angeles, I gradually became aware that someone was looking at me. Keeping my head facing my computer, I swivelled my eyes around the cabin until I was sure. Yes, I was definitely being watched. It was the woman from across the aisle, and she was making no attempt to hide it. In fact, she was being quite overt about it, using that gaze we all use when we want someone to put down their work and look up. I am not very chatty on planes at the best of times, but I am particularly unresponsive after delivering a speech. Since I had just given a two-hour talk, and since I had no idea who she was, I decided to make like a turtle. I hunched my shoulders, pulled my head in, tilted it forward, and began to type, hard.

"I'm a twenty percenter," she said.

I pretended not to hear. The engines were just noisy enough for me to have plausible deniability, so I didn't feel too bad about it. Unfortunately, she said it again.

"I'm a twenty percenter."

I may be unresponsive, but I am not rude, not often anyway. So I looked up.

"I'm sorry?"

"I'm a twenty percenter."

"Er, yes, I heard what you said, but I'm not sure I understood what you meant."

"I was at your speech. The one you just gave."

"Oh."

"Remember, you said that according to Gallup research only twenty percent of people report that they are in a role where they have a chance to do what they do best every day, and that the rest of the working world feels like their strengths are not being called upon every day. Remember, you said what a shame it was that so many people felt out of place in their work, and what a waste it was."

Of course I remembered. Ever since I learned of this statistic two or three years ago, I haven't been able to get it out of my mind. I included it in the first chapter of *Now, Discover Your Strengths,* and it still intrigues me. On one level it is sad that so many people feel miscast, but, on another level, what a wonderful untapped resource for any manager or company insightful enough to use it.

"Well," she continued, "I just wanted to let you know that we do exist. I have been working for the same company for the last two decades and I absolutely love what I do. Every day I get up and have the chance to express the best of me. I am one of your twenty percent. I'm a twenty percenter."

If you're in my line of work, no matter how tired or reserved you are, you don't pass up opportunities such as this. Here was a representative of a rare and valuable species, sitting right there next to me, obviously wanting to talk about it, and no distractions for the next four hours. So I shut down my computer, shifted in my seat to face her, and settled in.

"What exactly do you do?" I asked.

## DAVE, MYRTLE, AND TIM

> *"What does sustained individual success look like?"*

There are twenty percenters. And then there are the rest of us. At least, on some days, this is how it feels. The twenty percenters are those few individuals who, by dint of their ability, hard work, persistence, contacts, and yes, some measure of good fortune, manage to experience extraordinary, repeated, and sustained success. They choose wisely early in their careers and then, as the years go by, they build on their early successes, navigating around life's obstacles, or bulldozing through them, or clambering over them, making one right move after another, in a seemingly unending series of smart bets and excellent performances. And, strangely, they are not worn down by their efforts. Rather, as their careers progress, they actually seem to get better. They become more creative, more resilient, more expansive, as though somehow they have found a way to transform the friction of life into a perpetual motion machine of success and fulfillment.

All of which is more than a little intimidating to the rest of us. The rest of us tend to be much less consistent in both our achievements and our satisfactions. We begin our careers uncertain what our contribution will be, and although we become more focused as we gain a measure of self-awareness, as the Gallup data shows, alarmingly few of us actually wind up in positions where our contributions are at their peak. And even when we do experience success, many of us suffer from what has become known as Imposter Syndrome, the suspicion that we are not as good as everyone says we are, that our successes may have been accidental, and that, consequently, we may not be entirely sure how to repeat them.

For most of us, the eighty percenters, life really can seem, in Samuel Butler's famous phrase, "Like playing a violin solo in public and learning the instrument as one goes on."

Which is why surrounding yourself with a few twenty percenters can prove so valuable. There may be occasional twinges of envy at their success, their seeming serenity, their sense of direction, but, for the most part, they serve as inspiration. We know that life is never going to recast itself to our specifications, but these twenty percenters show us that, despite life's intransigence, and it's all too frequent attempts to drag us off track, it is still possible to find a way of engaging with life that is both predictably productive and consistently fulfilling.

I don't know how many twenty percenters you have in your life. I have three. Three, anyway, whom I would like to introduce you to, since the question here is "What is the One Thing they know about sustained individual success that the rest of us have forgotten, or perhaps never knew?"

### *Dave*

Recently I sat down to lunch with Dave Koepp. On the surface, Dave is not particularly remarkable. His Banana Republic shirt and chinos, his sandy brown hair of sensible length and cut, his bemused chuckles at the challenges of raising his two boys, the self-effacing way he describes his achievements, everything about him says Middle America.

Only his passionate defence of the Green Bay Packers— "They would have won the game if Philadelphia hadn't completed on fourth and twenty-six. Fourth and twenty-six! No one completes on fourth and twenty-six!"—stands out, clueing you in to which part of Middle America he hails from: Wisconsin. Pewaukee, Wisconsin, as it happens.

But, in Dave's case, first impressions are misleading. Dave Koepp is a twenty percenter. He has done something all of us aspire to, yet very few achieve. In his chosen field—one, mind you, that is littered with the defeated and the desperate—he has found lasting success and satisfaction.

In high school, despite his love of the Packers, Dave opted for drama class over sports. Today he explains this choice as part of a well-thought-out dating strategy—"In high school sports the boy-to-girl ratio is terrible, but in drama class . . ." he says with a grin. On closer questioning, though, he concedes that there was more to it than that. He had always loved movies, and drama class gave him the opportunity to indulge his fantasy that one day, after high school, after college, he would go to

Hollywood and become an actor. Then, one afternoon while watching *Raiders of the Lost Ark* for the umpteenth time, he was struck by the realization that films had writers.

"It was that scene where Indy's chasing after his girlfriend through the streets of Cairo and he is suddenly confronted by a villain with a very big scimitar. This guy slashes his weapon side to side, up and down, grinning like a maniac, and Indy has this whip, right, his famous whip, and so you start thinking that you're in for one hell of a great whip-against-scimitar fight. Instead, Indy just reaches into his belt, pulls out his gun, and shoots the guy. It was great. Everybody loved it. We were all prepared for a great fight scene and instead Indy just shot him. And for some reason, the thought popped into my head, Someone wrote that. Some writer somewhere had figured out how to play with our expectations by setting up one thing and then delivering another. I don't know why this idea that movies had writers had never occurred to me before, but it hadn't."

Ironically, Dave later found out that, in fact, this scene was completely unscripted. A marvellous whip-against-sword fight scene had indeed been written, but on the day of filming, Harrison Ford came down with stomach flu, and so the director, Steven Spielberg, simply improvised a much shorter version of the scene in order to get Mr. Ford back into his sickbed as quickly as possible.

Regardless, from this moment Dave knew that he wanted to be a screenwriter. After escaping Pewaukee by way of the University of Minnesota, the University of Wisconsin Drama Department, and UCLA film school, he and a producing partner cobbled together the money to get his first cowritten script made, a mood piece set in Buenos Aires called *Apartment Zero*. Although the movie made little money at the box office, the critics were impressed, and soon he received an offer from Universal Studios to buy his second script, a yuppie thriller called *Bad Influence*. They were willing to pay him a significant sum, almost enough to recoup the money he'd sunk into the first film. But, as usual in deals between novice writers and monolithic studios, there was just this one thing they wanted him to do: in this case, rewrite the movie as a buddy comedy. "Which was ridiculous," says Dave. "I am not that interested in writing buddy comedies. Never have been. I find I am drawn to darker themes like paranoia, betrayal, control, or the lack of it. So, although I desperately needed the money, I decided to reject their offer."

Turning down a major studio in a town as cliquey and connected as Hollywood is not normally career-enhancing, so at this point, with one small movie made and one big studio rebuffed, the smart money was that he would slide down into the obscurity that awaits most wannabe screenwriters.

But Dave didn't slide. The executive whom he had rebuffed, impressed by his artistic integrity, hired him to write for the studio full-time and exclusively. (This sounds far-fetched, I know, but stay with me. It gets even more improbable.) Now happily ensconced in his very own office on the studio lot, Dave proceeded to become one of the most prolific and successful screenwriters in Hollywood.

The highlights: His next movie, *Death Becomes Her,* with Meryl Streep and Bruce Willis, was a bona fide commercial success, followed by *Jurassic Park,* which was, of course, a proverbial blockbuster. Then there was *Carlito's Way* with Al Pacino, the sequel to *Jurassic Park, The Lost World,* a little Tom Cruise vehicle called *Mission: Impossible,* the psychodrama *Panic Room* with Jodie Foster, and in 2002, *Spider-Man.* As I am writing this Dave has just finished the screenplay for Steven Spielberg's latest project, *War of the Worlds.*

In Hollywood, no one is supposed to have this kind of success. Only a tiny percentage of scripts are sold. Out of those sold, only a slightly higher percentage are made into films. And out of those made, only one in a hundred takes in more than $50 million at the box office. In the face of these odds, Dave's achievement—seventeen movies made, 35 percent over $50 million and 24 percent over $100 million—is absurdly unlikely.

And the wonderful thing about Dave is that, despite his success, he still seems just as giddy about writing and making movies as he was twenty years ago. After getting his boys off to school, he can't wait to shut himself up in his office, put on the headphones, turn Springsteen up loud, and disappear into whichever world he happens to be creating. "Writing the first draft is always my favourite time," he says. "Nobody is giving me notes, informing me that this is good and this isn't. Nobody's intruding. It's just me and my characters, telling our story. I can't imagine anything more fun."

Of course, this picture of Dave is incomplete. I have not described any of the annoyances that drive him batty: the chattering executives who "know better", the studios who back out of their commitments at the last minute, or any of the personal burdens he bears. All of these are a part of his life, as they are, in whatever form they happen to take, for the rest of us. What impresses me about Dave, and why I keep him in the top of my mind when I am thinking about sustained individual success, is not that his life is perfect. Rather it is that he has somehow found a way to sustain passion, spirit, and superior performance despite life's imperfections.

## Myrtle

Myrtle Potter has managed to do the same, albeit in an utterly different field. She grew up in Las Cruces, New Mexico, where her father took out a second mortgage on the house in order to send her to an out-of-state college, the University of Chicago. After trying, disliking, and quitting a sales management role with Procter & Gamble, she was hired on as a sales rep by Merck, where she did so well so quickly that within a few years she had been called up to headquarters and put on the fast track.

Although pleased with her progress, she soon realized that Merck actually had two fast tracks. Track A (Myrtle's label, not Merck's) offered you deep-dive experiences into the challenges of selling pharmaceuticals and lofted you, hopefully, to the top sales role in a division, the regional director role. Track B provided a much broader range of experiences, such as forays into market research, pricing, and business development, and culminated, all being well, in a general management role running one of Merck's divisions.

The moment she perceived this split, Myrtle knew she wanted to be on Track B. Although she was good at sales, she found herself intrigued by the broader business questions, such as: How should this drug be marketed? What medical evidence will we need to reinforce our marketing positioning? What pricing levels will this drug support in the marketplace? And since these were precisely the kind of questions that Track B would prepare her to answer, she had to get onto Track B.

Merck thought otherwise. They kept her glued to Track A, and quite soon, because of her continued success, they offered her the regional director role. So Myrtle turned them down.

"They were shocked," she recalls. "You have to understand that for thousands of people at Merck this regional director role was the be-all and end-all. It was the job everyone was supposed to want, the job that some people waited fifteen years to get. No one turned it down. And yet here I was, a young black woman still in her twenties, refusing to take the job. I explained my reasoning, that I wanted to learn to look at the business holistically and maybe run a division one day, and that I didn't think the regional director role, with its exclusive sales focus, was the right fit for me. But no one seemed to understand. I think they saw me as a naïve young thing who, over time, would come to her senses."

So they kept offering her the position and she kept turning them down. This standoff continued for a couple of years, until, reluctantly, they gave her a bone. At first sight, it didn't appear to be much of a bone. She was asked to join a team putting together a joint venture between Merck and Astra, and, once this was done, to then lead the team charged with branding, pricing, and marketing the drug at the centre of this joint venture. This was a drug for treating acid reflux disease, and the bad news was that, despite ample clinical evidence of its effectiveness, it wasn't selling well. In fact, it was selling so poorly that both

Merck and Astra set up a deadline: either the drug would hit a certain sales volume by this deadline or the partnership would dissolve.

"By the time they moved me into the leadership slot, things were moving so slowly that nobody thought I would hit the deadline," Myrtle remembers. "I even wondered whether they had given me this assignment because they thought I would fail, and then I would learn my lesson."

Needless to say, she didn't fail. Instead, she did something quite extraordinary. She launched the drug, Prilosec, on a trajectory that took it from a nonstarter selling at a rate of a couple of hundred thousand dollars a year to, eventually, the highest-selling drug in the world. When she said this during our interview, I automatically scribbled it down in my notepad. Only a couple of seconds later did it fully register.

"I'm sorry. Did you just say that Prilosec became the highest-selling drug in the world?"

"Yes."

"This isn't just a figure of speech, right? You meant to say that Prilosec sold more than any other prescription drug in the world?"

"Yes."

"How much is that in actual sales volume?"

"About four billion dollars a year."

"Just so that I understand correctly, you're saying that you took this drug from a couple of hundred thousand a year and set it on a course to ultimately reach over four billion dollars?"

"Yes."

And so, the obvious question: "Er, what did you do?"

A book could probably be written on the subtleties of what Myrtle and her team did, but, as with most strokes of genius, the essence of it is really quite simple. She began by talking to the customers, which, in Prilosec's case, were the doctors who for some reason were opting not to prescribe it. She wanted to know why.

Apparently, they didn't think they needed to. They knew that Prilosec worked to cure the symptoms of acid reflux disease, but they thought that, for the majority of patients, it was unnecessary. Instead, they began by prescribing a class of drug called H2 antagonists, such as Pepcid, Zantac, or Tagamet. Only those patients who didn't respond to this regimen—a minority of patients—were eventually prescribed Prilosec.

So Myrtle led her team back to the New Drug Application files and, after sifting through forests of clinical trial data, they discovered two critical facts relating to Prilosec. First, that whereas Pepcid, Zantac, and Tagamet alleviated a patient's symptoms, Prilosec actually cured the condition and left the patient symptom-free. Second, that a certain kind of patient with a certain configuration of symptoms would never respond to the other drugs, and that in the end, whether it took six months or eighteen, this patient would wind up being given Prilosec.

Armed with these insights Myrtle went back to her doctors and asked, "What if I could define for you a certain kind of patient who will never benefit from the other drugs, who will only ever be rendered symptom-free by Prilosec. Would you be willing to prescribe Prilosec immediately, rather than using it as a drug of last resort?"

The doctors said they would. At this, Myrtle reworked all the marketing materials and trained all the salespeople to make these two points—only Prilosec can leave a patient symptom-free, and with a certain kind of patient, Prilosec should be a first resort, not a last resort.

A couple of months later, sales began to explode. Prilosec beat its deadline with three months to spare. Merck and Astra formed a separate company devoted to selling Prilosec. And Myrtle won Merck's coveted Chairman's Award.

As I describe all this now, her insights and actions seem so obvious, you have to wonder why nobody had thought of them before. But as I said earlier, most things that work perfectly appear obvious in hindsight. The trick is to have the talent to see in advance what is obvious, and then to act on it.

Myrtle undoubtedly has this talent. She continued deploying it to great effect at Merck, and, for a couple of years, at Bristol-Myers Squibb, until finally the biotech giant Genentech called and asked her to come and be its chief operating officer. Today she is its president. Still passionate, still intense, still insightful, and, with 20 percent growth each of the last four years under her belt, still hugely successful.

### Tim

Tim Tassopoulos completes my trio of twenty percenters. Looking for a summer job after high school, Tim went to the local mall, applied at a couple of retailers, and then wandered down to the food court and bought a Chick-fil-A sandwich for lunch. Somehow he got talking with the owner, who promptly hired him. Tim wasn't one of those food lovers who can't imagine working outside of a restaurant, but, as he says, "I worked hard, and I liked serving people, so all in all I think I did a pretty good job those first couple of months."

Tim must be understating things a little, because his new boss was so impressed he saw fit to call up the founder of Chick-fil-A, Truett Cathy, and suggest that it would be worth his time to meet this new recruit. Apparently it was, because from that meeting on, Truett became personally invested in Tim's success. He invited Tim to come to Chick-fil-A's annual meeting as a special college guest. He took him to new store openings around the country. He gave him internships during his college summers and made sure that he was charged with meaningful assignments. Most important of all, Truett expressed his confidence that Tim had the talent and the character to become the kind of steward-leader who would lead his company into the future.

This was heady stuff for a young college kid. Tim was thankful for Truett's confidence and felt at home in the overtly spiritual culture of Chick-fil-A, but he remained uncommitted, uncertain of how he should direct his energies. The countervailing influence was his love of politics. He was majoring in political science and was so taken with his subject that he didn't yet feel able to succumb to the lure of business. So, as a compromise, he decided to head off to Georgetown to pursue his MBA. The MBA would satisfy his interest in business; Georgetown, located in the heart of Washington, D.C., his interest in politics.

And there, at Georgetown, a mile from the Hill, he made a discovery. When his friends, like his roommate, George Stephanopoulos, described what they were doing during their internships with lawmakers, lobbyists, and political action groups, Tim found it all wholly uninteresting. Not boring, per se; just uninspiring. Initially he couldn't figure out why. They were at the centre of things, weighing in on matters of great import, forging relationships with some of the most powerful people in the country. How could this not stir him up?

Only after listening to their passion and comparing it to his own complete absence of passion did he realize what was wrong. This is how he describes it today: "I wanted to influence people. And I wanted to do it right now, today. I wanted the immediate feedback of making a difference in a particular person's life. Working behind the scenes in politics, there is a great deal of people contact, but you don't actually influence people. You influence *policy*. And, even worse, the pace of your influence is glacial. I just couldn't stand it."

So, having graduated at the top of his class, he left the rarefied air of Georgetown and returned to Atlanta, Georgia, and the relative obscurity of Chick-fil-A. Six years ago, after a speedy career progression from district manager—a role Chick-fil-A labels "business consultant"—to regional executive, to vice president of stores, he was promoted to senior vice president of operations for all of Chick-fil-A's twelve hundred stores. In this role he is charged with coaching, guiding, and influencing the heads of field operations, operations services, purchasing and distribution, human resources, and training and development.

Given Chick-fil-A's growth (a 50 percent increase in stores over the last six years) and its increasing visibility within the industry (when Tim assumed his SVP role they were ranked by Quick Service Restaurant magazine as the twenty-third most popular drive-through in America, whereas for the last three years they have been ranked number one), Tim is very much in demand in the executive job market. However, when head hunters try to get in touch with him he doesn't even take their calls. "How could I possibly find a better situation than the one I am in now? In Chick-fil-A I have a company that believes in me, that challenges me to give of my best every single day, and that puts me in direct contact with wonderful people who expect me to help them and guide them and coach them every day. In so many ways, I am blessed."

• • •

So, what is it with Tim, Myrtle, and Dave? Or if you don't relate to these three, what is it with the twenty percenters in your life? Why have they been able to achieve such sustained success? And how come they are still so happy in their work? "Happy" is not quite the right word, is it. It's a more nuanced feeling than mere happiness. How come they are still so "intense yet fulfilled"? Or perhaps "focused yet inquisitive" is better. Or "relentless yet passionate". Whichever word combination you prefer, if you know any twenty percenters, you'll get what I am driving at. These people are excellent in their chosen field, but they are not content. They are bodies in motion, proud, for an instant, of their laurels, but immediately willing to trample on those laurels as they step up to the next challenge, and the next.

As Butch said to Sundance, looking back at the pursuers who just kept on coming, "Who are those guys?" And even more important for our purposes, "How can we become them?"

From my research, the difference between the twenty percenters and rest of us can be found less in what they choose to do and more in what they choose *not* to do. Time is an annoyingly inelastic resource. You can't slow time down, or speed it up, or stash some of it away, or buy more of it. When confronted with a resource as scarce and inflexible as this, twenty percenters are rigorously discriminating about how they choose to deploy it. No matter how tempting the offer, they refuse to get sucked into activities that, on some visceral level, they know they will not enjoy. Thus Dave rejected the offer to write buddy comedies. Myrtle turned down all those job offers. Tim looked politics in the eye and decided that it would crush his spirit.

Either subliminally or consciously, they remembered the One Thing we all need to know to sustain our success:

## Discover What You Don't Like Doing
## and Stop Doing It.

Your strengths—your love of problem solving, your intuition, your assertiveness, your altruism, your analytical mind—are your natural appetites, and are, in this sense, irrepressible. I say this because your strengths are not only activities for which you have some natural talent; they are also activities that strengthen you. When using them, you feel powerful, authentic, confident, and, in the best sense, challenged. As such, they are self-reinforcing. Left to their own devices, they will, they must, be expressed.

What makes sustained success so elusive is that, unfortunately, your strengths are rarely left to their own devices. After you have employed your strengths and achieved some initial success, other people—often well-meaning people, but, more often than not, people who are unaware of your strengths—

insist on offering you new opportunities, new assignments, new roles. Some of these may call upon your strengths, but many will not. The secret to sustained success lies in knowing which engage your strengths and which do not and in having the self-discipline to reject the latter.

If your strengths are those activities that strengthen you, your weaknesses are the opposite. They are activities that weaken you. Confusingly, you may experience some achievement when using them—Myrtle was quite an effective salesperson—but, in spite of this achievement, they leave you feeling depleted, drained, frustrated, or merely bored. To sustain success in life, you must recognize these weaknesses for what they are and ruthlessly eradicate them from your life. In this sense, success is less about accumulating and more about editing. The metaphor here is not building, but sculpting, in that sustained success is caused not by what you add on, but by what you have the discipline to cut away.

To bring this discipline to mind, stop reading for a moment and try to recall an event in which you struggled. It doesn't have to be a significant, career-threatening failure, just some event where things didn't work out the way you wanted them to. Now, sit back and reflect on this event. Walk through it in your mind in as vivid detail as you can. Identify which aspects of this event were within your control. What did you not do that in hindsight, you should have done? What little mistakes did you make that if you were to do it all over again, you would avoid making? Have you made these mistakes before? Is there a pattern here?

If so, why do you always seem to struggle in these kinds of situations? Do you lack the talent to see what needs to be seen?

Or do you possess the talent but lack the ability to become energized and excited by these kinds of situations? Do they bore you, or frustrate you, or drain you of energy? Do they, in the end, leave you feeling empty?

Obviously, I have no idea what you are thinking about. But I can tell you that your sustained success depends on your ability to reflect on events such as these, to use them to identify those things that weaken you, and then, as efficiently as possible, to cut these out of your life. The more effective you are at this, the more successful you will be. Freed from the friction of these things that weaken you, you will then be able to unleash fully the power of your strengths.

On the surface, this advice—"Discover what you don't like doing and stop doing it"—seems superficial or incomplete. Whatever happened to paying your dues, or stretching yourself with new and difficult assignments, or balancing your life with some things you like and some you don't? And what about the intrusion of real life? Yes, it would be nice to orient your life away from those activities you don't like doing, but who has that luxury? Surely, you have, and will always have, some aspects of your work that bore you or frustrate you.

These are sound questions. To answer them and, in the process, to reveal the full power of the One Thing, we need to return to the beginning of the journey and examine the other explanations that had to be considered before "Discover what you don't like doing and stop doing it" emerged as the most incisive and the most practical insight.

## THE EARLY CONTENDERS

*"What explanations seem like the One Thing, but aren't?"*

Let's begin with the most easily dismissible explanations.

For obvious reasons, sustained success has nothing to do with age, sex, race, or religion.

Education may have something to do with it, but education alone is not the answer. All of us know well-educated people who have found neither success nor satisfaction in life.

It's not hard work. Of course, all twenty percenters do work hard, but so do countless others who are not nearly as amply rewarded for their diligence. So yes, hard work is necessary for sustained success. But it is not sufficient.

How about risk-taking? Dave certainly took a big risk by moving out to Hollywood with no money and no contacts and by rejecting Universal's offer to buy his second script and turn it into a comedy. Myrtle took many a risk by turning down all those promotions. But Tim? Not much evidence of risk-taking there. In fact, you could argue that, by returning to the Chick-fil-A fold, he opted for the safest of all routes. So risk-taking is not the answer.

You may worry that my three twenty percenters are not representative of the world at large, that I am, in fact, committing the sin of generalizing from the particular. If so, bear this in mind. Risk-taking is one of the most frequently and most reliably measured personality traits. Today, there is a growing consensus in academic circles that virtually all personality traits can be boiled down to five, labelled mundanely the Big Five.

Two of the Big Five are openness to experience, which basically measures how intrigued you are by novelty and variety, and extraversion, which measures how much external stimuli or excitement you crave. In combination, they form a good proxy for risk-taking. And yet despite hundreds of studies examining the role of these two traits in performance, no reliable link has been found between either one and sustained success.

The other three traits are neuroticism, how highly strung you are; agreeableness, how accommodating you are; and conscientiousness, how organized and methodical you are. And in case you're wondering, no reliable links have yet been found between these three traits and sustained success. This doesn't mean that we have discovered all there is to discover about the role of personality in sustained success. Entrepreneurs may, and I stress *may* because the results are hardly conclusive, possess more extraversion than the norm. Applied scientists may be more conscientious than theoretical scientists. The average artist may be more open to experience than the average accountant. But these findings, such as they are, only refer to a person's likelihood to pursue certain types of career, not to whether this person will experience sustained success in that career. So, as things stand, it's fair to say that the "all twenty percenters share the same personality traits" explanation is a red herring.

How about interest, plain and simple? Perhaps those who happen to find a field in which they are instinctively, deeply interested are more likely to achieve and sustain success. Well, Dave is certainly interested in movies, as Myrtle is in healthcare, but, again, Tim confounds this explanation. He is both productive and fulfilled despite not being what those in the restaurant trade call a "foody". Think about your twenty per-centers for a moment. Is each of them deeply interested in the field in which he has experienced his success? I imagine that many of them are, but I bet that one or two will remind you of Tim, someone who is successful in his chosen field, but who could probably have been just as successful in any number of different fields. Interest per se, while obviously valuable, is nei-ther necessary nor sufficient to explain sustained success.

What about sheer talent? Dave, Myrtle, and Tim are clearly talented in their chosen roles, although Dave's talent is a matter of opinion—there's no arguing with his box office, but you may not have liked what he did with *Jurassic Park*.

But regardless, is talent really the One Thing that can ex-plain their sustained success? I don't think so.

Just to be clear, I am a huge fan of the concept of talent and am certain that a person's talents—defined as his recurring patterns of thought, feeling, or behaviour that can be produc-tively applied—do play a significant role in performance. If you are naturally assertive you will be more likely to succeed in sales than someone who shies away from confrontation. Like-wise, if you are naturally vigilant, your chances of succeeding in the police force are higher than if you are oblivious to your surroundings. And since a person's talents do not change signif-icantly after you hire him, there's little doubt you would be wise to select people whose talents match the demands of the role.

But selecting for a role with a close eye on talent, whether your own or a new recruit's, won't guarantee sustained success. It is merely one, albeit important, step in the journey. Even if you are a twenty percenter yourself, the chances are that you know a lot of people whose talents match their roles, but who nonetheless struggle to sustain extraordinary levels of performance and fulfillment.

Why does this happen? Basically, because talent describes potential, not performance. If you possess the talent to ask "what if?" questions and to construct contingency plans, you have the talent, the potential, for thinking strategically. This is a wonderful gift—think how hard it is to train someone to be strategic if he doesn't possess this talent to project into the future vividly and accurately. But the presence of this talent doesn't tell us anything about whether he will be able to acquire the requisite technical knowledge, or find the right situation, or build the right relationships so that he can deploy it, or whether he will be able to summon the will and the enthusiasm to deploy it consistently. Talents, correctly identified, reveal a person's capacity. They don't guarantee his success.

These early contenders fall easily with a few quick jabs. But ahead, we are going to meet three explanations that are much more plausible, and that in some cases contain powerfully useful insights. To evaluate them, we are going to have to get more precise about what we mean by sustained success.

## WHAT IS SUSTAINED SUCCESS?

*"It's a broad term. How do we*
*define it?"*

Obviously, each person is driven by his own particular definition of success. For our purposes, though, I am going to hang my hat on this one:

# Sustained success means
## making the greatest possible impact
### over the longest period of time.

Broad as it is, this definition accommodates our diversity. Some of us yearn for prestige, others for expertise, and still others for the satisfaction that comes from being of service. Some of us value family above all else, while others are prepared to sacrifice time with family for the sake of career advancement. Some of us define success only through our achievements at work, while others are more inspired by their contributions to their church, their synagogue, their community, or their country. But no matter where we choose to direct our energies, no matter what audiences we choose to play to, no matter what markers we use to measure our progress, our goal must surely be to have the greatest impact possible for the longest period of time. Only then will we be deemed successful.

This definition doesn't refer to money or title or recognition, although, presumably, no matter what your field, if you have a significant impact over a long period of time one or all of these will be forthcoming. It refers simply to your ability to make a significant contribution and sustain it.

Armed with this definition, our question changes from "How can you become like Dave, Myrtle, and Tim?" to "How can you have the greatest possible impact over the longest period of time?"

Actually, we can be even more specific. To have a great impact over a long period of time requires two things of you.

First, it requires that you take your natural talents and your enthusiasm and apply yourself to learning enough role-specific skills and knowledge to be deemed good at something. This, in and of itself, can be quite a challenge, but, annoyingly, good is always relative. If you are good at something and everyone else is better, then you are no longer good. Therefore, success doesn't just mean learning role-specific skills and knowledge. It also means targeting your learning toward those areas where you possess some kind of comparative advantage over everybody else. The more of a commodity you are, the less successful you will be. Or, as Peter Drucker once said, "Something special must leave the room when you leave the room."

Second, this definition of success requires that you not only get good at something, but that you stay good and more than likely get better. To stay good and get better places some special demands on you, particularly since change, in the form of new products, new competitors, new processes, and even new laws, has the alarming habit of quickly rendering your carefully crafted expertise obsolete. To survive in these "times of great change"—another Drucker phrase—will therefore demand that you be resilient, flexible, open to learning, innovative, confident, optimistic, and, all the while, sufficiently devoid of stress to maintain your energy for the long haul.

So where does this leave us in the search for the controlling insight? The controlling insight, the One Thing, must first tell you how to deal with those aspects of yourself that make you different from everyone else, and then it must show you how to be resilient, creative, and serene enough to win, and keep

CHAPTER 6

# The Three Main Contenders

## CONTENDER 1

### *"Find the right tactics and employ them."*

The premise of this school of thought is that your success has little to do with overarching concepts such as talent or intelligence. Instead, no matter what your talent or intelligence, success results only when you employ the right tactics. Go to the self-help or career section of your local bookstore and you will be overwhelmed by the volumes of tactical advice available.

Here's a sampling of three of the best. First, consider Tony Schwartz and Jim Loehr's book *The Power of Full Engagement*. Tony and Jim studied highly successful athletes—initially tennis stars, as it happens—and discovered that the most successful players did not have measurably better ground strokes or serves. Sure, each player had his own particular strengths and weaknesses, but every player good enough to make the ATP tour had the ability at crunch time to launch a massive serve or fire a cracking forehand down the line. Counterintuitively, what differentiated the best from the rest was not what happened during the points, but rather what happened *between* the points. The best had faster and more effective recovery routines. In the thirty seconds between points, the best players were able to slow their breathing and their heart rate dramatically, thus recovering the energy and the focus they would need during the subsequent point.

Tony and Jim have since applied this insight to the corporate world, telling us that the best way to succeed is through a disciplined process of stress and recovery. Stress itself is not the enemy we typically think it is. Uninterrupted stress is. So look at your life as a series of sprints, they say, rather than a marathon. Impose on your life a set of routines that allow you to stress yourself, then recover, stress, then recover, and you will find that, over time, your capacity, your resilience, and your energy will all expand.

They apply this to all forms of energy—mental, emotional, spiritual, and physical—and offer up some very practical routines you can immediately install into your working life. For example, they tell us that since the human body is designed to work most effectively in ninety-minute increments, you should discipline yourself to get up after an hour and a half's work and walk around, breathe deeply, take a break. No matter how engaged you are in finishing a project or writing an e-mail, when the ninety-minute bell sounds, stop your work, walk around, breathe deeply, take a break. I've found this to be extremely valuable advice. In fact, I am trying to discipline myself to write this book as a series of sprints. I don't know if it will make the book any better, but it sure seems to leave me with more energy at the end of the day.

James Citrin and Richard Smith in their book *The 5 Patterns of Extraordinary Careers* are even more specific in the tactics they suggest. They are both executives at the recruitment consultants Spencer Stuart, and so presumably they have seen a lot of successful careers in their day. As part of their advice, they tell us that to "build our personal brand" we should "go blue-chip early." Translation: regardless of your long-term career plans, join a large, well-known company early in your career—because all companies, large or small, tend to be risk averse and therefore are much more likely to hire someone whom a blue-chip company has already deemed worthy.

Apparently we should also avoid what they call the "permission paradox." Translation: you can't get the job without the experience, but you can't get the experience without the job. Therefore you should proactively seek out special projects and one-off assignments because these will allow you to claim that you have skills and experiences not supplied by your current job.

And then there is David D'Alessandro's book *Career Warfare*. As the title suggests, he takes a more combative approach. It's a highly competitive world out there, he says, and the more successful you are the more competitive it becomes; the ladder gets narrower, the slots fewer. So in order to win the career war, there are certain tactics you must discipline yourself to employ. For example, you should proactively manage your boss by providing him with the three things he really wants—loyalty, good advice, and a subordinate who will never make herself look good at his expense.

You should deliberately make friends in high places, because you never know when you will need their help to circumvent a particularly self-serving boss who insists on taking credit for your achievements.

And most important, remember that, in D'Alessandro's words, "It is always Showtime.

"No matter what transaction you think is occurring during your workday, and no matter how trivial and boring it appears, there is always another transaction taking place that is about *you* and the impression you are making. Unfortunately for their careers, most people pay very little attention to the way they handle the mundane stuff. They have the mistaken idea that the only thing that matters is landing the client, not being pleasant to the boss's assistant on some ordinary morning."

As you can see, some of D'Alessandro's tactics are commonsensical. Some of them are less so—a section on why you should avoid working for entrepreneurs is quite surprising (apparently entrepreneurs will become jealous of your success). But there's little doubt that most of these tactics, when applied at the right time and in the right way, can help you succeed.

So, if the best of these tactics are both well thought out and practical, why isn't "Find the right tactics and employ them" the One Thing you need to know about sustained individual success? Simply because "Find the right tactics and employ them" doesn't tell you how to avoid becoming a commodity. You are different from everyone else. You have different strengths, weaknesses, interests, background, and experiences. If there is one thing the One Thing *must* do, it must tell you what to do with this unique mix of resources. It must make your individuality its focus.

The next two contenders do precisely this, although their perspectives on what you should do with your individuality are diametrically opposed.

## CONTENDER 2

### *"Find your flaws and fix them."*

I confess that I don't have much sympathy for this one. I have touched on it in previous books, and the only reason I bring it up again is that, unfortunately, it remains the most commonly held view around the world. According to Gallup data, a majority of Americans, Brits, Canadians, French, Japanese, and Chinese all believe that fixing their flaws is the best strategy for sustained success.

Its basic premise is this: although you possess a unique complement of strengths and weaknesses, your greatest room for growth lies in your areas of weakness. So, in order to succeed, you must identify your weaknesses and work to improve them.

This is how Larry Bossidy and Ram Charan describe it in their book *Execution:* "If you sit down with your boss and your boss hasn't said something to you about your weaknesses, go back! Because otherwise you are not going to learn anything."

The *Harvard Business Review* even offers you a preferred

sequence for how to go about fixing your weaknesses: "Start with the flaws that prevent [you] from achieving minimal performance standards for key tasks. When you've taken care of those, move on to the weaknesses that are preventing [you] from advancing [your] career" (*HMU,* June 2002).

Not only will this diligent weakness-fixing make your boss happy—nothing pleases a leader more than seeing a subordinate honestly confronting his weaknesses and then working long hours to improve them. But it will also, apparently, increase your chances of sustaining your success. The thinking here is that, in these times of rapid change, the only way to avoid being rendered irrelevant is to learn as many skills as possible. If you're good in sales, learn marketing, finance, and operations. If you excel at process design, be sure to study human relations and public speaking. If you're the ultimate tactician, take a strategy course. The more skills you learn, the more well-rounded you will become, and thus the greater your likelihood of survival.

Dr. Mike Lombardo, previously of the Center for Creative Leadership, labels these skills "career freedom options", or CFOs. Here's his take on CFOs from his book *The Leadership Machine:* "We would suggest that your happiness, fulfillment, and the extent to which you can follow your dream at any stage of your career is determined by your CFOs. The more you have, the happier you can be. . . . The more CFOs you have in the bank, the more opportunities there are, and the more choices you can make. . . . Building CFOs is career enabling. Not building them is career chilling."

Another cited benefit is that pushing yourself to overcome

your weaknesses is actually quite energizing. Your weaknesses are those things you find difficult, but the good news, according to this school of thought, is that what is difficult is also challenging, and so your weaknesses cry out for attention if you want to stay challenged. Or as Dr. Richard Boyatzis, coauthor of *Primal Leadership,* describes it: "If you don't stretch people, they will ultimately get bored with their jobs and leave" (*HMU,* June 2002).

Dr. Lombardo is even more explicit on this point: "Essentially, development is the land of the first-time and the difficult. Comfortable circumstances applying skills we already have not only do not lead to growth, they lead to stagnation and retirement in place." The most successful people, he says, possess something called learning agility, defined as "the willingness and ability to learn new competencies in order to perform better under first-time, tough or different conditions. Learners are willing to go against the grain of what they know how to do and prefer to do. Why? To get better and to learn new skills and new ways of behaving."

From all this, it's clear why "Find your flaws and fix them" holds such universal appeal. It will keep you challenged. It will keep you nicely well rounded. It will keep you humble. And perhaps most important, it will keep your boss happy.

And, to its credit, it does deal directly with the two requirements I set up earlier for sustained success. First, it tells you what to do with your unique complement of strengths and weaknesses: maintain the former and fix the latter. Second, it tells you how to sustain your success for the long haul: acquire as many "career freedom options" as possible.

So, with all of this going for it, why isn't "Find your flaws and fix them" the One Thing you need to know about sustained individual success?

Well, the most obvious reason is that, despite its appeal, few successful individuals subject themselves to it. (This is not to say that successful individuals have closed their minds to learning new things. On the contrary, most of them are inquisitive types, always intrigued by the chance to learn new skills and see new perspectives, and some work in extremely dynamic fields, such as computer graphics or applied science, where such openness to new information is a prerequisite for survival. The point is simply that they choose not to target this inquisitiveness toward fixing their flaws.) Not coincidentally, few successful managers subject their people to it. And few successful teachers subject their students to it.

But this isn't actually a very good reason. It begs the question "Why?" Why do the most successful individuals, managers, and teachers choose not to invest their time in finding flaws and fixing them?

The most up-to-date research yields two answers, one biological, one emotional. The biological answer reveals that you will not, in fact, learn the most in your areas of weakness. The emotional answer states that you will not in fact feel most energized and challenged when fixing your flaws.

### *You will not learn the most in your areas of weakness.*

In this section we're going to dig into the biological underpinnings of learning with a view to answering four critical questions:

- What, if any, are the limits to what you can learn?
- Why are some things easy for you to learn, while other things are excruciatingly difficult?
- Does learning slow down during the course of your life?
- And the big one: as an adult, where are you likely to learn the most?

Before we answer these questions, a word of advice: if this section promises more biology than you had expected from this book, or if your own experiences have already convinced you that you will not learn the most in your areas of weakness, you may want to skip ahead to page 243. However, if you have the kind of mind that always seeks the root causes of things, you may find this next section intriguing.

Have you ever wondered what happens in your brain when you learn something new? I mean physically, not philosophically. What physical thing or substance changes when you learn how to pronounce the word *Saskatchewan,* or how to boil an egg, or how to connect a face to a name? You probably know how your muscles grow—when you exercise you cause microscopic tears in the muscle, and as the muscle repairs itself over the next day or so, it becomes stronger, more massive. But how does your brain grow?

If we can get right down to the actual biological processes that drive learning we may be able to answer those four questions.

Over the last decade it has become fairly common knowledge that learning is determined by the intricate network of connections between your brain cells, or neurons. Your brain is constructed of a mind-bogglingly large number of neurons—the estimates vary, but a conservative figure would be twenty billion. These neurons don't do the learning for you, though. This task is accomplished by a little something called a synapse. To get one in mind, imagine a long, thin wormlike thing sticking out from your round-shaped neurons. Some of these synapses (the axons) send signals away from the neuron toward other neurons, while others (the dendrites) are designed to do the opposite. They receive signals from other neurons. Whether you are one day old or sixty years old, the process of learning occurs in exactly the same way. One neuron sends out a signal through its transmitting synapse, and over in a different area of your brain, another neuron picks up this signal through its receiving synapse. During the course of your life each neuron will forge tens of thousands of these synaptic connections with other neurons, and with each new connection one new snippet of information is learned.

All this is accurate, as far as it goes, but it is not particularly enlightening. Pinpointing the synapse as the seat of learning doesn't actually enable us to answer our four questions. It simply changes the language of the questions a little bit. Our questions now become:

- What, if any, are the limits to the number of synaptic connections you can forge?
- Why are some connections easy for you to forge, while others are excruciatingly difficult?
- Does synaptic connecting slow down as you get older?
- And, as an adult, where will you forge the most synaptic connections?

To find the answers we will have to delve down one level below the synapses, to the agent that actually causes your synapses to fire in the first place: namely, to your genes.

Science has already reaped many benefits from the recent mapping of the human genome—gene therapy and prenatal genetic screening, to name two—but, for our purposes, one of the most intriguing results was the discovery that our genes are the real workhorses of learning. A gene is a particular stretch of DNA whose main job, it appears, is to make a protein. You have roughly thirty thousand genes, and each gene encodes the recipe for a protein. There are currently quite a few metaphors floating around for explaining the chief function of a gene—it's a blueprint, a storage system, a language—but the one that has been the most helpful to me is the "it's a switch" metaphor. So, think of a gene as a switch, with two settings, on and off. When it is switched on the cell dutifully makes the protein the gene codes for, which then launches a chain reaction of ons and offs. The protein expressed by the first gene serves as the instruction to another gene down the line to switch on and make its own protein, which in turn causes another gene to switch off and stop making its protein, which in turn causes another gene to switch on, in an endless cascade of instructions.

This cascade of ons and offs tells each cell in your body what to be—to become hand cells at the extremities of the arms, skin cells on the surface of the body—and then instructs each cell what to do once it becomes specialized. In your brain, this means that your genes not only guided the initial development and wiring of your neurons before birth, but, now that you're an adult, your genes continue to serve as the active agents in determining which of your synapses will fire, when they will fire, and how often. Or, more simply, when one neuron reaches out and forges a synaptic connection with another neuron it is only because one of your genes told it to. Matt Ridley, in *Nature via Nurture,* paints this vividly: "Right now, somewhere in your head, a gene is switching on, so that a series of proteins can go to work altering the synapses between your brain cells so that you will, perhaps, forever associate reading this paragraph with the smell of coffee seeping in from the kitchen."

In other words, what you can learn and what you can't is determined by what genes you have.

This doesn't mean that experience has no part to play in learning. On the contrary, experience, or "nurture", plays a significant role in determining which neurons fire and which don't. Rats raised in highly stimulating cages—lots of wheels and mazes—wind up with many more synaptic connections than rats left in barren, boring cages.

But it does mean that how and what you learn from experience is determined by your genes. For example, no matter how much experience you are given, you will never learn to smell as effectively as a rat. Why? Because a rat has 1,036 different olfactory receptor genes, whereas you have only 347. Similarly, no matter how much we try to teach chimps language, they will never be able to speak like us. Why? Because although the human and chimp genomes are 98.5 percent identical, in an area of the genome closely connected to language acquisition, labelled CpG islands, the chimp's genes differ from ours by 15 percent. A few special chimps may be able to learn the odd bit of sign language, but when it comes to complex syntax and grammar, they just don't have the genes for it.

In one sense, then, a species can be defined by what its genes allow it to learn. You can say the same thing about a person. Your genes are 99.9 percent the same as mine, which explains why we can both learn to speak, to reason, to feel remorse, to grieve, and to back our cars out of the driveway. But the 0.1 percent difference between our genes is not insignificant. In the brain, these slight differences will cause a few of your genes to switch off while mine are still on, which in turn will cause a multitude of other on/off differences further down the cascade, thus ensuring that not only will your brain be wired a little differently at birth than mine, but, even more important, your brain will learn differently than mine as you grow.

If you think that I am taking too great a leap from genes to something as complex as personality and learning, consider this example, again from *Nature via Nurture.* Each human being possesses a gene for making a protein called BDNF. This protein seems to act as a sort of "fertilizer in the brain encouraging the growth of neurons". A small percentage of people possess a tiny mutation in this gene (if you're interested in the specifics, the 192nd position in the gene is adenine, whereas with most people it's guanine) which, all by itself, causes an entirely different protein to be built. When measured on personality profiles, those with the mutated gene are significantly less depressed, self-conscious, anxious, and vulnerable than those with the regular version, and, intriguingly, they also score much higher on certain memory tests.

Obviously, I am not suggesting here that a certain gene automatically creates a certain trait or learning ability. But I do want to show you how one minuscule difference in the sequence of one gene out of thirty thousand can, via the subsequent cascade of genetic ons and offs, produce measurably different personalities. Matt Ridley puts it even more bluntly: "Neither I nor anybody else can yet begin to tell you how or why a tiny change results in a different personality, but that it does so seems almost certain. A change in a protein recipe can indeed result in a change in personality."

One way to test this would be to alter a person's genes and see whether his personality and style of learning changes. Of course, ethics forbids anyone from trying this on humans, but a few fascinating experiments have been conducted on the lowly flatworm, the fruit fly, and the mouse, and the findings confirm the causal link between genes and personality. For example, flatworms with one version of the gene *npr1* tend to be social, while those with a slightly different version of the gene are loners—they stick to themselves when foraging. By altering this gene, geneticists at the University of Toronto have managed to turn socials into loners and vice versa. In a similar vein, researchers at the National Institutes of Health have created a strain of anxious, fearful mice by simply knocking out one particular gene that produces a protein for transporting serotonin.

All of this research reveals that you are stuck with, or blessed with (depending on your perspective), your unique complement of genes and the distinct learning and memory patterns they create. Obviously, this doesn't mean you can't learn. Even the flatworm, with only 302 neurons and no discernible brain, can be taught to prefer a certain temperature if it is repeatedly fed at this temperature. What it does mean, though, is that you will learn slightly differently from me, because your genes are slightly different from mine.

Thus far I think we've answered the first two questions. Your genetic makeup explains both why there is a limit to what you can learn (since you don't have the genes of a rat, you'll never smell as well as a rat) and why some things are easy for you to learn, while other things are excruciatingly difficult (you always excel at remembering people's names because you have the genes for it, but you always struggle with analyzing data because you don't).

So, let's move to the last two questions.

Does learning slow down during the course of your life? The simple answer is yes. It takes significant resources to forge new synaptic connections—genes have to be turned on, proteins created, synapses fired, blood vessels built—and nature is not in the habit of wasting resources unnecessarily. Consequently, once connections have been forged, your brain is designed to protect these connections by insulating them with a substance called myelin. This protection ensures that you don't have to keep relearning things you've already learned, such as eye-hand coordination or the name of your mother. But this myelin coating is not without its costs. It actively hinders synaptic growth. This is why a very young monkey, whose left eye has been covered with a patch, can regain the use of the covered eye when the patch is removed, but an adult monkey cannot. It is also why brain injuries suffered in adulthood prove much more persistent than those suffered in childhood, and why learning a foreign language is much easier at five than it is at thirty-five.

This is not to say that all synaptic connecting stops after adolescence. In a series of famous experiments, people who became blind as adults and who had to learn Braille were found to have significant synaptic growth in the areas of their brain dealing with touch and synaptic depletion in those areas dealing with sight. But it does mean that, when you reach adulthood, your brain is much less malleable than it was in childhood, and therefore that, when it comes to learning, your adult brain will always be looking for the least biologically costly way to forge new connections.

This answers the final question: As an adult, where are you likely to learn the most, or, in biospeak, where are you likely to see the greatest growth in your synaptic connections? Since the least biologically costly way to forge new connections is to piggyback on connections already in place, you will actually grow the most new connections in those areas of your brain where you already have the most existing connections. In the words of Joseph LeDoux, a professor of neuroscience at New York University, "Added connections are therefore more like new buds on a branch rather than new branches."

This has huge implications for your learning. As an adult, you will not learn the most in areas that are new, different, difficult, and against your grain. You will learn the *least* in these areas, and what you do learn will be achieved inefficiently. Circumstances may sometimes require you to do this—one person may quit the team, leaving you to plug the gap and get up to speed as fast as possible. But be sure to see this for what it is: a brief distraction from the real focus of your learning.

Most of your learning should be targeted toward those areas where you have already achieved some level of mastery. If you have a natural ability to solve problems, or to build relationships, or to compete, or to anticipate the needs of others, you will get the most bang from your learning buck from stretching, refining, and focusing these abilities. In these areas of mastery, your synaptic branches are already in place. Here new buds of learning will flourish.

### *You will not feel most energized and challenged when focusing on your flaws.*

Take a moment to think about an activity at which you excel. It doesn't much matter what it is—it could be something at home or at work—just make sure it's an activity in which you have developed a level of mastery.

How do you feel when you anticipate performing this activity? How do you feel during the activity? How about when you've just finished it?

The chances are that, if you are like the rest of us, the state you're thinking about right now will be some combination of self-confidence, optimism, positivity, and a feeling of being in control. We often call this state self-assurance. Cognitive psychologists label it self-efficacy.

Self-efficacy is not the same as self-esteem. Self-esteem refers to your general feeling of worthiness, and, while having high self-esteem must, in some general sense, be a good thing, unfortunately a recent study in the U.S. sponsored by the American Psychological Society revealed that high self-esteem predicts nothing at all—not resilience, not persistence, not goal-setting, and certainly not achievement.

Self-efficacy is not a general feeling, but rather is always tied to a specific activity. You might have feelings of high self-efficacy for selling computer software, or for administering injections safely, or for analyzing corporations' annual reports. And, in contrast to self-esteem, your level of self-efficacy for an activity does an excellent job of predicting your subsequent performance. It predicts how quickly you will bounce back from failure at the activity, how forcefully you will persevere at the activity when you meet obstacles or setbacks, how high your goals for that activity will be, and, most important of all, the likelihood you will actually achieve these goals. When it comes to performance, self-efficacy is one of the most powerful of mental states.

Although your self-efficacy is tied to specific activities, it does come in very handy when you are confronted by new challenges. According to research by Albert Bandura, past president of the American Psychological Association, how well you face new challenges is determined by your ability to transfer your self-efficacy from one activity to another. The best way to do this is to look deliberately for similarities between the new challenge and previous challenges where you have succeeded in the past. The more similarities you find, the more you feel able to maintain your high level of self-efficacy, and therefore the more resilient you are, the more you persevere, the higher your goals are, and the more likely you are to achieve those goals.

So, if you want to sustain your energy and enthusiasm from one challenge to the next, the absolute worst thing you can do is to leap far away from your comfort zone and into something that is entirely different from those activities where you have already developed mastery. Great enthusiasm and success do not occur in the land of the new, the first time, the different. The exact opposite is true. Great enthusiasm and success occur in the land of the familiar and the similar. The more similar a new challenge is to one of your existing areas of mastery, the more likely you are to learn quickly, to persevere, to set high goals, and to achieve them.

Before we move on, consider one other discovery about the role of emotion in sustained success.

In the previous chapter I asked you to recall an event in which you struggled. Now, I'd like you to do it again, but take it one step further. If you can stand to, think back to an event in which you not only struggled, but one in which you failed, utterly and publicly. What did you fail to do? How did it make you feel? Try to re-create your emotions as vividly as you can.

Heaven knows what's in your mind right now, but it's a safe bet that I am starting to put you in a bad mood. Good. This was the point. Now, quickly, see how many other negative events you can recall. They don't have to be the same kind of event as the earlier one, just any negative events. They can be related to work, home, school, anything, just so long as they're negative.

Perhaps you should write them all down, but don't feel compelled to do so. It may be too depressing. However, if you were a volunteer in my study you would indeed be asked to write them down. And what I would find is that, having put you in a bad mood, you would be able to recall significantly more negative events than you would if your mood was neutral. Likewise, if I put you in a good mood—by telling you to think about a recent success or to imagine what it would feel like to win the lottery—you would be able to remember significantly more positive events.

This study has been repeated many times over, with different cross sections of volunteers, and the results are always the same: the more an event matches your current mood, the more likely you are to recall it.

The way cognitive psychologists explain this is that when an event occurs, you store in your memory not only the specifics of the event (your boss walked in just as you lost your place in your presentation and you had to start over) but also how this event made you feel (incompetent). Over time, as more events occur, you build up a network of event memories all connected by the fact that they created in you a similar emotion. So when a new event occurs that makes you feel just as incompetent as you did when your boss walked in, the entire network of events-where-you-felt-incompetent lights up, making it almost impossible for you to not think about them. In Albert Bandura's words, "Activating a particular emotion unit in the memory network will facilitate recollection of events linked to it." Or in common parlance, negative moods will activate thoughts of past failings, whereas positive moods will activate thoughts of past successes.

Some in the academic community believe that the power of your mood extends even further. Professor J. D. Teasdale's research has led some to the conclusion that negative moods don't just activate memories of specific failures in the past, but, more worrying still, they activate a global view of oneself as worth-less and inadequate.

Well, okay, but I don't think we need to weigh in on this ac-ademic debate, because, for all practical purposes, it amounts to the same thing. Forcing you to think deeply about a specific fail-ure in the past has significantly negative repercussions for you. This is how Bandura describes your downward spiral: memo-ries of negative events increase despondency, and "despon-dency lowers self-efficacy beliefs; the lowered beliefs, in turn, weaken motivation and spawn poor performance, breeding an even deeper despondency in a downward cycle."

So if you really want to ruin your chances of sustained suc-cess, ponder your weaknesses, ruminate on your past failings, chew on your flaws. Pretty soon you'll wonder why it's worth getting out of bed in the morning.

• • •

Let's take stock. From all this research we now know that your genetic makeup, although very similar to mine and everyone else's, differs from the rest of ours in small but meaningful ways. We know that these genetic differences cause your mind to become wired with a unique network of synaptic connec-tions, which, in turn, creates in you distinct patterns of thought, feeling, learning, memory, and behaviour. We also know that while you will continue to learn throughout adulthood, you will learn the most in those areas where you already know the most, where your synaptic branches are already thick and strong.

On the emotional side of things, we know that you will be more likely to be resilient, persistent, self-confident, and effective in those areas where you have developed some mastery, and you will transfer these powerful feelings to new challenges only if these new challenges are substantially similar to your existing areas of mastery.

Finally, we know that you will feel more positive and energized when you avoid thinking deeply about past struggles and instead focus your mind on past achievements. Or, as my mentor Dr. Donald O. Clifton was fond of saying, we know that "you are never as strong as when you have clearly in mind your successes."

All of this would seem to lend significant support to the last of the contenders for the One Thing: "Discover your strengths and cultivate them." This is undoubtedly a powerful insight, which should inform many of your choices, especially early in your career. However, as we'll see, it does not quite go far enough. It sets in motion a series of consequences that it then fails to address.

## CONTENDER 3

*"Discover your strengths and*
*cultivate them."*

Take a moment to follow Don Clifton's advice. Think back to a recent success and get it in mind as clearly as you can. What caused this success? More than likely a few external factors played a part, such as timing, a happy combination of circumstances, luck. Cut through these if you can and examine the role of your own behaviour. What did you actually do that enabled good things to happen?

Did you prepare particularly carefully? Did you analyze all the variables at play and see with great clarity which combination of variables would lead to the best outcome? Or did you just act faster and more incisively than others would have done?

Maybe your success can be explained less mechanistically. Maybe it had less to do with clear thought and clear action and more to do with your intuition—on a gut level you just knew what you had to do. Or maybe your empathy and your sensitivity explain your success—your own actions were less influential than other people's willingness to help you. Or perhaps you were simply more persistent than everyone else.

When you land upon a satisfying explanation, think back to another success and see whether you can apply this same explanation. Then try another. And another.

There are many formal ways to discover your strengths—the StrengthsFinder profile, the Myers-Briggs Type Indicator, the Kolbe profile—but I have found that this kind of first-hand reflection on past successes can serve as an excellent starting point. The more you investigate your past successes, the more you'll recognize that certain recurring patterns of behaviour or perception always seem to crop up. If you can get enough distance from yourself, you'll see not only that these patterns are a consistent part of your personality—you're always competitive, or focused, or patient, or conceptual—but also that you're most successful whenever these patterns mesh perfectly with the challenge facing you.

These patterns are your strengths, and since they are a function of the way your brain is wired, you are likely to be blessed with them your entire life. Over time you may learn to channel them more productively and deploy them with greater sophistication, but you are not going to change them significantly. In fact, as I've just described, current brain science suggests that during the course of your life they will become ever more pronounced, that strong synaptic branches tend to become stronger still, and that, in this sense, growing up means becoming more and more of who you already are.

Given all this, there's no question that identifying your strengths and orienting your career around them is sound advice. In my interviews I have met hundreds of people who have done precisely this, but, among all of them, I've found no better life story than Tami Heim's to reveal the power of building your career around your strengths. For reasons I'll describe in a moment, it is rarely easy to keep your strengths front and centre, but somehow Tami makes it look almost effortless.

Tami always had a fascination with stores. So great was her fascination that by the age of twelve she knew she wanted to go into retail.

She smiles. "Actually, that's not entirely true. I started playing store with my friends much earlier than that. But it was only when I reached twelve that I started talking about it seriously."

At sixteen, urged on by her uncle, she put her fascination to the test by applying at a Lazarus department store in her home town of Indianapolis. They said that they weren't hiring any part-time people, but because Tami had no idea what part-time meant, she just sat in the waiting room all day in the naïve hope that her obvious passion would get her hired. And, as happens in stories like hers, when she was finally granted an interview with the operations manager, her passion did indeed win him over.

She was asked to report to the stockroom the next morning.

"Initially they gave me all the rotten jobs to show me that real-life retail wasn't the same as playing store, but what they didn't realize was, from that very first day, I was addicted. I'm the sort of person who focuses on the present, on the now, on the 'What can we do today?' question, so I loved the immediate feedback of retail. If you decide to change this display, or move this item from one section to another, you can tell right away whether it worked. The results are instantaneous. And I loved the theatre of it, the drama of putting on a show every day for thousands of customers. I just couldn't imagine anything more exciting than coming in every day and having the chance to do that."

She worked at the store all the way through high school, through her college years studying retail management at Purdue University, and upon graduation was hired into their management training programme. The next fifteen years saw her move up through the management ranks, from department manager, to store manager of a small store, to a larger store, and then on to regional vice president. Progress wasn't always as smooth as this sounds—her company, Federated Department Stores, entered bankruptcy midway through this period, which, among other things, resulted in Tami's being shipped off for an eighteen-month posting to a store three hours away from her young daughter. But, through it all, she maintained her passion for the drama, the relationships, and the immediacy of retail.

And then Borders called. Would she come and be one of their territorial vice presidents, responsible for the western United States? Although this would mean that the family would have to move to Michigan, that her mother, suffering from Alzheimer's, would have to move with them and live in their home, and that her research scientist husband would have to put his career on hold to care for her mother, she weighed it all up and took the job.

Two years later the chairman of Borders led her into his office and told her that the board had met and decided that, in one year's time, she would be made president. They were a little concerned that her only experience was store operations, so during the year prior to her assuming the presidency, she was made senior vice president of sales, marketing, store planning and design, and café operations. It was the first staff job of her career, the first time she would have no profit and loss responsibility.

"How did you take to it?" I asked.

"Oh, it wasn't too bad," she says. "Because, you see, I had such a rich understanding of operations, I already knew how sales, marketing, and design were supposed to come together in the store. I viewed operations—what the customers actually saw in the store—as the integrating point for all the other disciplines. So, although I never became an expert in any of them, I looked at them through the lens of 'how will this help operations' and I think this caused me to stay focused and make good decisions. Besides, I knew I was only going to be in this role for a year."

When the year was up, she was duly elevated to the presidency, a position she has now held for four years—from her perspective, four fantastic years.

"Every day I get to come in and play this huge game of store, selling a product I love to customers who really want it and surrounded by a fantastic team of colleagues."

Borders isn't complaining either. During her tenure, despite excellent competitors, foreign wars, and the Internet debacle/opportunity, profits have grown consistently and so has the stock price—up 66 percent since 2002.

Tami's story is impressive, even inspiring. Would that we could all experience such success. I am not referring to her climb up the corporate ladder, simply to her ability to find a series of roles that played to her strengths so consistently.

However, I didn't highlight Tami in order to lend weight to the notion that "Discover your strengths and cultivate them" is the One Thing you need to know about sustained success. Instead, I picked Tami because she is an exception. She is not a twenty percenter. She is, if you like, a one percenter, a person who was able to find her strengths' track and stay on it, with no distractions, diversions, or temptations for her entire career.

Hers is a singularly unusual situation. Much more common are situations where you find a role that plays to your strengths, where you duly experience some success, and then because of this success, new opportunities, new roles and responsibilities are thrust in front of you and you have to choose among them. Many of these prove tempting, but only a few of them will actually allow you to continue using your strengths. The rest look innocuous enough, but they will actually start to drag you off your strengths' path.

Usually, this doesn't feel like a wrenching switch. You are rarely going to make drastic career moves, from nursing to journalism, say, or from sales to operations, and if you do you will tend to keep your senses finely tuned to whether the new role is indeed the right fit for you. Instead, what usually happens is career-creep. Following your initial success, one new responsibility is added, then another one, then another, as your job slowly shifts beneath you, inching you farther and farther away from your strengths' path until, finally, you wake up one morning and realize that the majority of your job now bores you, leaves you unfulfilled, frustrates you, drains you, or all of the above.

To sustain your success, it is imperative that you keep yourself alert to these subtle changes and take immediate action to correct your course. If you don't, you will wind up so far off track you might never find your way back.

I'll use myself as an example. I joined Gallup because I wanted to learn how to build interviews to measure a person's talents. Once there, though, I realized that what I truly loved was explaining to clients the awesome power of talent. Sure, the intricacies of interview design held a certain fascination, but it was nothing compared to the thrill of trying to make sense of a complex phenomenon like talent and of standing up in front of a sceptic and attempting to get him to see what I could see. I wasn't always successful, of course, but this didn't weigh on me much. Each person's reaction revealed a little more about which of my examples resonated and which didn't, where my logic flow was intuitive and where it was convoluted, and I used these insights to practise and to tinker. I became quite good at my job and yet still remained passionate and inquisitive enough to stay late at the office scribbling new ideas and diagrams on the white board and pacing the stage of the empty auditorium, listening to myself say the words out loud.

At this point in my career, I had all the markings of a bona fide twenty percenter.

And then, imperceptibly, things started to change. One of the clients whom I persuaded to see and act on the power of talent was a large entertainment company. Facing new competition, they were looking for anything that would give them a sustainable competitive edge. Gallup's offering—a systematic way to select more talented employees—seemed to fit the bill.

The engagement began with a series of presentations to their directors and managers on why talent was important and how to select for it. Twice a week for months and months, hundreds of employees would file into one of their convention meeting rooms, whereupon I would jump up and give them my best Select for Talent speech. Things were going well, and I couldn't have been happier.

In fact, things went so well that, over time, the size of the engagement grew considerably. More and more Gallup consultants became involved, delivering an increasingly complex series of programmes and products, and in order to ensure the quality of a relationship I had worked hard to build, I moved to Florida to help manage it all.

There in Florida, I was still expected to do a fair amount of explaining and presenting, but, below my radar, the managing aspects of the job were growing each day. I was so caught up in wanting things to succeed that I didn't consciously register the change. Besides, I was capable of handling the intellectual requirements of the role acceptably well, so alarm bells such as missed assignments or blown deadlines didn't blare a warning that something was beginning to go badly wrong.

What did slowly dawn on me was that my personality was changing. I was becoming irritable, quick to anger. I was tense all the way through a meeting and couldn't relax afterward. I would stay up at night going over and over each person's responsibilities and stumble out of bed the next morning ill at ease and distracted. My health began to suffer as the cocktail of little sleep and constant worry gradually wore me down.

After eighteen months of this, I was a mess.

The advice to "Discover my strengths and cultivate them" would not have shown me how to stop my slide. What caused my slide wasn't that I had somehow stopped using my strengths. On the contrary, even as I was sliding, I was still calling upon my strengths every day—during this eighteen-month period I made more than five hundred presentations on the power of selecting for talent.

Instead, what caused my slide was that my responsibilities had shifted so dramatically that the *majority* of my job now involved not presenting, but a whole list of other activities, such as being immediately available and responsive to the client's needs, being responsible for the quality of other people's work, and juggling many different projects at once. For reasons that relate back to my genes and my synapses, each of these activities confused me, took their toll on me, and, in combination and over time, drained me of energy. It wasn't that I had been Peter Principled—no one had promoted me to my level of incompetence. It was just that my initial success had caused many new doors to open and I had unwittingly walked through all of them.

In short, my problem wasn't that I was so far off my strengths' path that I couldn't find any success. My problem was that, having found success, I didn't have the discipline to stay focused when faced with the increased complexity and opportunity that success brings.

The One Thing you need to know about sustained individual success—**"Discover what you don't like doing and stop doing it"**—confronts this issue directly. Yes, you should start your career by taking stock of your strengths and orienting your career choices around them. And yes, as you experience some measure of success, you should feel free to experiment, to try new roles and responsibilities and see how they fit. However, as you grow, as you experience success, you must keep your senses alert to those aspects of your role that bore you, or frustrate you, or drain you. Whenever you become aware of some aspect you dislike, do not try to work through it. Do not chalk it up to the realities of life. Do not put up with it. Instead, cut it out of your life as fast as you can. Eradicate it.

If I had kept this One Thing front and centre I would not have wasted eighteen months of my life. Instead, I would have taken steps (which I'll describe in the next chapter) to remove these activities from my life, leaving me free to cultivate and refine my unique areas of strength.

"Discover your strengths and cultivate them" is then sound advice, but it is incomplete. To use a sports analogy, it will get you in the game. But the initial success it causes sets off a series of repercussions—more opportunities, more complexity, more choice—which, if you are not careful, will prove extremely unproductive for you.

"Discover what you don't like doing, and stop doing it" tells you how to handle these repercussions. Once you're in the game, it specifies the discipline you will need to reach all-star levels of performance, to sustain those levels, and to win, consistently.

• • •

As you strive to apply this insight, you will undoubtedly hear dissenting voices.

Some people will tell you that it doesn't matter whether you like your work; you just have to be good at it. Question this advice. You may well be good at some activities you don't enjoy, but your enjoyment is the fuel you require to keep practicing the activity, to keep stretching, investing, and pushing yourself to greater levels of mastery. Lacking this enjoyment, your performance will likely plateau.

Some people will tell you to be suspicious of those activities you enjoy because you just might love an activity you're bad at. Obviously, this does sometimes happen. You only have to watch the outtakes from the television show *Pop Idol* to see legions of people who love to sing but who are unaware of the distress they cause when they do. And, yes, this can happen in the workplace—I used to work with someone who kept volunteering to make presentations even though his voice and cadence were as sleep-inducing as *Guess How Much I Love You.*

However, it actually happens less frequently than you might think. If you aren't good at something, you will fail repeatedly, and, as Albert Bandura's research revealed, when you fail at an activity repeatedly, your self-efficacy for the activity falls, your level of despondency rises, and over time, simply as a self-preservation measure, you actively start to avoid it. Liking something you are bad at will always be a temporary state of affairs. (When it persists, it is usually because the person remains unaware that he's bad. This is a failure either of the performance measures or of how clearly those performance measures are being relayed to him. In which case, brutally honest feedback may be required.)

Some people will tell you that you need a little difficulty in your life, a little grit; that, as an oyster makes a pearl, this grit will strengthen you, round you out, and polish you into something fine and valuable. No grit, they say, no pearl.

Treat this advice sceptically. When it comes to your career, grit will only grind you down. Every minute you invest in an activity that grates on you is a poorly invested minute. It is a minute in which you will learn little and that will leave you weaker and less resilient for the next minute. It is a minute you could have spent applying and refining your strengths, a minute in which you could have taken leaps of learning and that would strengthen you for the minutes to come.

Some people will tell you that only those who are already successful have the luxury of cutting their dislikes out of their job. Again, be sceptical. They have it backward. People who are already successful became so precisely because they were unwilling to tolerate aspects of their job they didn't like. Their intolerance *caused* their success.

Of course, this is not to suggest that you should ignore the needs of your colleagues or refuse to chip in and offer support when asked. An approach as self-absorbed as this would surely make you very unpopular. The point here is simply that you will contribute the most, as either an individual performer or a team member, when your role closely matches your strengths, and that it's your responsibility to try to arrange your world so that it does.

To keep track of your effectiveness at this, every three months you may want to take a moment to write down your answer to this question: what percentage of your day do you experience a feeling of self-efficacy, that optimistic, positive, challenged-yet-confident, authentic feeling? Phrased more simply, what percentage of your day do you spend doing those things you really like to do?

Recently I attended a meeting at Best Buy, in which ten of their most sustainably successful store managers were asked this question. Their answers ranged from a low of 70 percent to a high of 95 percent. These numbers may seem unrealistically high to you, but they are consistent with the answers of the most successful people I've interviewed, and as such they should serve as your benchmark. The most successful people sculpt their jobs so that they spend a disproportionate amount of time doing what they love. This doesn't happen by accident. It happens because they stay alert to those activities they don't like and cut them out as quickly as possible. They jealously guard their "doing what I love" time.

To sustain your success, you must do the same. Be vigilant. Assess where and how you are spending your time. Yes, you should feel free to experiment with new roles, skills, and responsibilities, but the moment you perceive that you are spending less than 70 percent of your time on things you love to do, identify the activities getting in the way and take action to remove them. The more effective you are at this, the more creative, the more resilient, the more valuable, and thus the more successful you will be.

# CHAPTER 7

# So, How Do You
# Sustain Success If...?

And so the question begs: How exactly do you do it? How do you "Discover what you don't like doing and stop doing it?"

At first glance, the "Discover what you don't like doing" part seems rather straightforward—how hard can it be to realize that you don't like something?—while the "stop doing it" part is much more challenging. And, as regards the latter, you would be right. When it comes to removing aspects of your job you dislike, the world is set against you.

There's no doubt that organizations would benefit significantly from turning as many employees as possible into twenty percenters, but they are not actually set up to make this happen. They are set up, the good ones anyway, to deliver something valuable to a customer. Your success and fulfillment are of interest to them only insofar as what you are doing adds value to their customer delivery system. And the majority of organizations have decided that the most efficient way to ensure that you do add value is to define a standard version of each role—salespeople do W, sales supervisors do X, sales managers do Y, sales leaders do Z—and train you to fit as snugly as possible into these prefabricated molds.

Even the most overtly developmental programmes—such as the opportunity to work with a professional coach or to participate in a leadership training class, complete with 360-degree feedback tools and competency models—are, on close scrutiny, revealed to be elaborate attempts to plug your gaps and make you fit the role better.

As we've seen, the research record reveals that this kind of "be less of who you are" approach to development is counterproductive. However, there's no denying the sense in designing an organization to serve a customer. My point here isn't that this is wrong-headed. My point is simply that, when you work in an organization, you need to remember that eradicating your dislikes is not very high on anyone's agenda. When it comes right down to it, you're on your own.

Take heart, though. Eradicating your dislikes is not quite as daunting as it seems. Consider the first part of the One Thing, the "Discover what you don't like doing" part. This actually requires a little more thought than it appears to. All dislikes are not created equal. Each dislike, each thing that irritates has a different cause. You will find that the more carefully you identify the cause of your dislike, the better you will be able to determine what you need to do to eradicate it. I am not saying it will ever be easy, but at least you will be able to act with more precision.

A dislike is caused most often by one of four distinct emotions. Each of these emotions has, in turn, a different cause, and therefore each will respond to different interventions. The first two, as I'll describe, require the same drastic action. But the second two afford you a greater range of motion.

## YOU'RE BORED

If your overriding feeling is one of boredom, the chances are that your deep interests are not engaged. You may enjoy the activities themselves, but the content leaves you cold.

Melissa Thomas was in this predicament. When I met her, Melissa was the supervising producer of *Good Morning America.* She was the person who sat in the control room scanning twenty or so monitors that contained the various video clips, live feeds, and studio shots that would come together to make the show. It was her responsibility to sequence all of these shots so that you, the viewer, would see something coherent and entertaining.

And she was very good at it. She was not only adept at deciding how the story of a particular segment should be told, and at whispering just the right amount of information into the earpieces of the hosts, but she seemed to be at her very best whenever something went wrong. While most of us would panic if a satellite signal was lost or a studio guest froze on camera, Melissa became even clearer in her thinking. Somehow she seemed to have anticipated just such an eventuality and knew exactly which shot to cue up in order to cover the gaffe.

So, Melissa's problem wasn't that she couldn't do the job

well. Her problem was that she found the subject matter of a morning show unbearably tedious. She was interested in politics, economics, world events, and while a few segments were devoted to these, most of the programme consisted of lighter fare: a fashion show of Victoria's Secret's new spring line of bikinis; how to bake the perfect pumpkin pie for Halloween; an interview with the owner of this year's international dog show winner.

She suffered through her boredom for a little over a year, and then, having surveyed her options, she took the only possible course of action. She quit and sought out a role that engaged her interests more directly—in her case, this meant enrolling in Columbia's School of Journalism.

If you find yourself in a similar predicament, you will have to do the same. When the content of your job proves deeply uninteresting to you, you must change the job.

## YOU'RE UNFULFILLED

Sometimes your dislike stems not from a lack of interest, but from a lack of fulfilment. You may enjoy the activities of the job, and even perform them well, but your values are not engaged. The most obvious example of this—and we've seen plenty of them recently—is when your company, or your boss, asks you to do something blatantly unethical. Clearly, when faced with this situation, your only recourse, having made your disagreement known and seen no change in behaviour, is to remove yourself from the situation, which usually means quit the role.

Some examples, though, are less clear-cut. You know you are starting to find your work grating, but you have to examine your feelings quite closely before realizing that what's missing is the values component. This is what Catherine Davies did.

Today, Catherine is a key account manager for Charles Schwab, where she is responsible for managing the relationships with some of Schwab's high-net-worth clients. She has been in this role for four years now and loves the fact that it asks her to be directly available to her clients and immediately responsive to their needs.

This "client advocacy role", as she calls it, fits her strengths and values perfectly, and now that she is in it, it seems almost inevitable to her that she would wind up here. However, looking back, one can see that her career journey has been rather circuitous. She has a bachelor's degree in political science, a master's in sports management, and along the way she flirted with adding another degree in engineering, architecture, or business. Eventually, prompted by a stint at the Institute for Public Policy, she wound up in Washington, D.C., as the legislative correspondent for Congresswoman Karen Shepard out of the Second District of Utah.

Once there, she found that her interests were engaged (she had been intrigued by politics since her undergraduate days) and that her strengths were called upon (a legislative correspondent basically performs the same role as a key account manager except that she is the constituents' advocate rather than the clients').

What she hadn't counted on were the compromises that big-time politics demanded.

"As a legislative correspondent you see a lot of mail. And you know what your constituents are saying. You know what your constituents are asking for. And you know what your constituents elected you to do. But in order to get on, say, the House Finance Committee, you have to sign onto a bill that goes against what your constituents say. Of course, I knew that government was based on compromise, but I hadn't realized how brutal the compromises were."

You might think that Catherine was a little naïve. If so, she retains her naïveté to this day. "I am still," she says, "disheartened by the fact that people have to give up what they campaigned for and what they believed in in order to stay in office. That's really hard on me."

Plagued by the necessity for severe compromise, Catherine took the only course open to her. She left the Hill and sought out a role where her success would depend on her ability to keep her word and to forge lasting relationships on the strength of it: the key account manager role.

If your values are disengaged from or actively compromised by your work, you must do the same. To stay in it for the money or the security is, in the long run, a bad bargain. It will rob you of the best of you.

• • •

What happens if your interests and your values are both engaged, but your strengths are not in play? This creates a very different feeling: frustration.

## YOU'RE FRUSTRATED

As I described earlier, your strengths are irrepressible. The firing of your thickest branches of synapses is the cause of your strengths, and this firing creates a force that demands expression. If you are naturally empathic you can't stifle it. You can't make yourself not sense the emotions of those around you. Sure, you can learn how to channel this strength more productively, just as you can learn how to avoid situations where it becomes counterproductive for you to express it—for example, don't become a collections agent for a credit card company because it's hard to succeed in collections if you are forever empathizing with the person who is refusing to pay. But what you cannot do is shut it off completely.

At least, you can't for long. If your role represses your strengths, you may be able to hold them in for a short while, but every day the pressure builds and builds, until, like a cork from a shaken Champagne bottle, they burst out.

Should your feelings of frustration reach these levels, your only recourse is to find another role entirely, one that gives your strengths free rein. But, if you catch your frustrations before they reach the red zone, you will see that another, less drastic course of action is open to you: tweak your role so that a part of it plays to your strengths, experience some success, and then parlay this success into a new, changed role that plays to your strengths entirely.

This will demand from you persistence, and from your manager a willingness to experiment, as Brian Dalton's story reveals.*

When I first met Brian he was a regional sales manager for a large medical equipment company, which sold a range of different

---

* Brian Dalton is one of the few pseudonyms in this book.

products—hospital beds, scopes, cameras, blades. This was back in the early nineties, and at that time, the best way to sell one of these products was to go directly to the doctor who used them and persuade her that your scope or blade or bed was technically superior to your competitors'. You never sold on price because, back then, hospitals were reimbursed on a cost-plus basis—the hospital told the government or the insurance company what a procedure cost them, and, with a small profit margin added on, they were then paid the full amount. Within reason they didn't really care about the price. They cared about the technical capability of the product.

To sell in this environment demanded that you hire and develop talented young salespeople who were smart enough to learn the features of the products, sophisticated enough to build relationships with high-ego doctors, and powerful enough to turn these relationships into deals. And Brian excelled at this. He had a knack for picking good people and for applying to his sales team just the right combination of love and pressure. He was regional manager of the year four years in a row.

But despite his success, Brian was growing increasingly frustrated. One of his most dominant strengths was his ability to examine the various elements of a situation and to discern from these elements a pattern, or a set of concepts, that explained why things worked the way they did. He was an idea man, a deviser of new ways of looking at things, a "dream-weaver", as the company's president took to calling him. This is a rare and valuable strength, and what irked Brian was that, in his current role, he was not allowed to express it. The prospects were set, the products were set, the prices were set, and all he was supposed to do was to deliver to each prospect a salesperson who would pitch the set product at the set price.

Frustrated, and contemplating his departure, Brian became aware of a change in the landscape, a change that, properly exploited, could give full expression to this dream-weaving strength of his.

At first glance, the change appeared mundane. At the beginning of this century, the U.S. government decreed that, henceforth, hospitals would not be reimbursed on a cost-plus basis. Instead, the government would set the price for each procedure, as specified in their Diagnostic-Related Codes, and Medicare, Medicaid, and the insurance companies would reimburse only this exact amount, regardless of the hospital's costs.

What this meant to hospitals was unmitigated panic. Previously they had paid limited attention to their costs; now, suddenly, their costs would determine how much profit they could squeeze out of each procedure. This cost pressure is as old as business itself, but to hospitals it represented the dawning of a strange new world.

What this meant to Brian was opportunity. Immediately, he realized that the prospect had changed from the doctor to the chief financial officer. What the doctors thought of the products was now less important than what the chief financial officer thought of the price. Faced with this new reality, Brian did what all dream-weavers do: he took an intuitive leap. He knew instinctively that it would be suicide to get into a price war with his competitors, so instead he set his mind to pondering this question: Regardless of the products he was selling, or the price of those products, what could he and his company do to help his hospitals be more successful in this new, financially constrained world? If he could answer this question, he and his company would be perceived as advisors rather than mere salespeople.

"We shouldn't be selling product," Brian explained. "We should be figuring out how to help hospitals face their new reality. Of course, if we proved ourselves to be really helpful, who do you think they would buy their equipment from?"

First he experimented with financing. Rather than demand to be paid in full immediately, he would allow his hospitals to defray their costs over time. This flew in the face of his company's billing procedures, but his boss gave him the green light and allowed him to try it out with a couple of hospitals. These experiments worked so well, and the size of these financed contracts was so much larger than the regular ones, that pretty soon, in addition to his regional manager responsibilities, he was advising the entire sales force on how to present his company's financing options.

With these successes under his belt, Brian's mind kept churning. (He's the kind of guy who literally stands on his desk in order to see things from a slightly different angle and who books a train ride from New York City to Washington, D.C., simply in order to sit and mull over the germ of a new idea.) And quite soon he fell upon this insight: in one very limited sense, hospitals are like manufacturing plants. Each hospital comprises a series of interconnected processes, the end product of which is a healthy patient. Continuing with the analogy, he realized that if you want to run an efficient hospital you could do a lot worse than employ sound manufacturing principles, like, say, inventory control.

One of the biggest problems in hospitals is lost inventory. In a medium-sized hospital literally millions of dollars worth of saws, sutures, bandages, scopes, and cameras are misplaced every year. Not misplaced as in stolen, just misplaced as in "I have no idea where they've gone." A doctor borrows a scope for his private surgery and forgets to bring it back. A nurse, knowing that left unattended, stuff tends to walk away, decides to hoard her equipment in a secret stash so that she always has it when she needs it. This AWOL equipment is a massive inefficiency because hospitals wind up replacing equipment they still have.

To combat it, Brian found and licensed a technology that would install a tiny computer chip in each piece of equipment. This chip would serve as a locator device, enabling the hospital administrators to know exactly where every piece of equipment was at all times, or to track the equipment if, for some reason, it walked out of the building.

To sell a hospital on this inventory control system required an utterly different approach from simply selling one product. Given that the hospital's up-front investment ran into the millions, each sale became a conceptual sell where the salesperson had to position himself as an efficiency consultant, rather than a product specialist. But, as before, Brian's boss gave him the leeway to experiment, to train a bunch of new salespeople, and to send them off into the field. Again success was instantaneous and widespread. So widespread, in fact, that with twenty-five of these multimillion-dollar deals closed, and 62 percent revenue growth this year alone, Brian's company decided to create a new division, Strategic Sales, and install him as its head.

Today Brian is challenged—these deals are never easy to close—but he is no longer frustrated. As he says, "I love the way my job is now. The worst thing my boss could do is promote me."

What began as a sense of frustration and a few weird ideas has grown into an entirely new role, one in which Brian is now paid to weave dreams into deals. If you feel similarly frustrated, there could be a way for you to do what Brian did. Find a tiny stream in which your strengths can flow, and carve it into the Mississippi.

• • •

The last emotion, although potentially the most damaging, actually offers you the widest range of interventions. This emotion is caused not by a lack of interest, nor a lack of fulfilment, nor a repressed strength. Instead it is created when suddenly, or gradually, your job requires you to have strength where you have weakness. As I can attest, when you are asked every day to engage with the world in a way that is unnatural for you, when, every day, you miss things you should have seen, when, every day, you are confused by things that others find clear, it is a draining experience.

## YOU'RE DRAINED

What can you do? Well, I suppose you could opt for one of the actions I've already described. You could quit the role, or try to tweak the role so that less of it calls upon your weaknesses. But, if you catch yourself early enough, there are a couple of other options you can try.

First, and most obviously, you can find someone else to do what you hate to do. Such is the variety of the human race that for virtually every activity there is someone out there who is predisposed to get a kick out of it. I recoil at the thought of having to confront people every day, but you revel in it. I am inept when it comes to designing and implementing action plans, whereas you are at your best. I am the least organized person on the planet, while you whistle contentedly as you alphabetize your spice rack and colour-code your sock drawer. Since, on my end, each of these happens to be true, my sustained success in life will depend on my ability to seek out and partner with someone like you.

Look around you and you will notice how frequently success and partnership are seen in each other's company. Remember the Thomas Jefferson example from chapter 1, how he so loathed public speaking that he changed protocol so that, while he would always write his own State of the Union addresses—one of his most dominant strengths—he would have an assistant run down Pennsylvania Avenue and actually deliver the speech to Congress? (Ironically, this is the exact opposite of what happens today, where the "assistant" writes and the president speaks.)

Well, this is merely one example of Jefferson's sophisticated use of partnership during the course of his exalted career. The most famous example is the way he and James Madison played off each other. Jefferson was a conceptual man who was most comfortable listening to what the historian Joseph Ellis calls "the harmonious and agreeable" ideas in his head. As such, he despised the disharmony of real-world debate and the unseemly cut and thrust of party politics. "If I could not go to heaven but with a party, I would not go there at all" was how he expressed this dislike.

A politician who dislikes debate would appear to have a crippling weakness, but not if he partners with a man like James Madison. Although Madison was as intelligent as Jefferson, his mind worked differently. He was a precise thinker, a practical thinker, who enjoyed debate, at least in part because it enabled him to work through the details. He was not a volatile, emotive orator in the John Adams mould. Instead, he was calm, reasoned, erudite, and respectful. Somehow, with very little huffing and puffing, decisions seemed always to go in his favour. In Ellis's description, "Jefferson was the grand strategist. Madison the agile tactician. . . . He was prose to Jefferson's poetry."

Today, one can find many examples of Jeffersons who have found their Madisons. Here's a sampling from the information technology sector, compiled by the *Washington Post:* Steve Jobs and Steve Wozniak at Apple. Steve Case and Jim Kimsey at AOL. Jim Clark and Marc Andreessen at Netscape. Larry Ellison and Bob Miner at Oracle. And, of course, Bill Gates and Steve Ballmer at Microsoft.

Speaking of Bill Gates, a chapter on sustained individual success would seem incomplete without some mention of the most successful man alive today. Although he clearly has his faults, he is successful on so many levels—his personal wealth, the pervasive influence of his company's products, his $21 billion charitable foundation, his seemingly balanced family life—that you have to ask yourself, Why him? What has he got that the rest of us don't? He's smart but no more so than most

Ivy League graduates. He's hardworking and persistent, but so are millions of others. He's no more emotionally intelligent than the rest of us. In fact, with his aloofness, his shyness, and that peculiar hunched, rocking motion he often slips into, "emotionally intelligent" might not be the first words that come to mind. So what explains his outlandish success?

Here is one thought for you to consider. Bill Gates's true genius, the genius that differentiates him from the masses, lies in his ability to find just the right partner at just the right time. This genius might not always be conscious, but review his career and you will find that he is a serial partner-finder. It began with his closest childhood friend, Kent Hood Evans. Evans was as fascinated by computers as the young Gates, but he was, according to the writer Mark Leibovich, more "dreamy, dogged, and largely devoid of inhibition. . . . He pushed Gates to think big and take risks." We don't know more about what this partnership could have become because Kent Evans was killed in a climbing accident on May 18, 1972. But we do know that it left a profound impression on Gates. The science and maths centre he donated to his high school bears this dedication: "In memory of classmate, friend and fellow explorer, Kent Hood Evans."

"It's been nearly thirty years," Gates says today, "and I still remember his phone number."

Following his friend's death, Gates moved on to forge a partnership with another classmate, Paul Allen. They bonded over their intense interest in computing, and each served to egg the other on as they envisioned what this burgeoning technology could become.

Then there was the rather less heralded partnership with a

Harvard colleague, Monte Davidoff. In 1975, the same year they formed their consultancy, Micro-Soft, Gates and Allen holed up in a small apartment in Alberquerque, New Mexico, and brought in Davidoff to write a tricky but vital piece of code. Davidoff returned for another stint of code crunching in 1977 but became so put off by Gates's intensity, that in one of the least prescient decisions in career history, he turned down an offer to become Microsoft's third employee.

And then, famously, Gates sought out and hired (as employee number 24) Steve Ballmer. For the last twenty-five years, Ballmer has served as Gates's alter ego. As mentally agile as Gates and just as hardworking, Ballmer nonetheless brings different strengths to the partnership. He is more extraverted than Gates, louder, more emotive, more willing to let others see his passion. Since he is also, like Madison, more tactical than Gates, he was the perfect choice to become Microsoft's CEO when in January 2000, Gates decided to return to his true love, strategic design.

Some may offer the challenge that "of course he can find the right partners. He's Bill Gates." But, as I mentioned earlier, the causal arrow actually goes the other way. He is "Bill Gates" in part because he had a genius for finding the right partners.

Whatever your assessment of Gates, when faced with a role that repeatedly calls upon your weaknesses, you would do well to remember that effective partnering is the quiet secret of the successful.

Failing this—if your Madison proves elusive, or if the activity that weakens you is too central to your role to hand off to a partner—there is one final intervention you can try: find an aspect of the activity that brings you strength and always keep this aspect at the top of your mind. This intervention involves more mind games than the others, but in some instances it is the only option available.

Cast your mind back to Dave Koepp, the prolific Hollywood screenwriter. Although writing is his first love, he has occasionally branched out into directing. He currently has three films to his credit: *Trigger Effect,* which examines the growing tensions caused in one suburban home when the electricity in Los Angeles is cut off; *Stir of Echoes,* which deals with creepy goings-on underneath Kevin Bacon's house; and *Secret Window,* which deals with equally creepy goings-on in and around Johnny Depp's up-country cabin.

Since he also wrote the scripts for these films, and since each of them deals with the same dark subject matter covered by his other scripts, Dave's approach to taking on new challenges is textbook perfect. He has not leapt into "the new, the first time, the different." Instead, as the self-efficacy research would have advised, he has sought out challenges that involve the overwhelmingly familiar, leavened with the ever-so-slightly different.

While this is all to the good, the roles of writer and director *are* different, and one or two of the director's responsibilities do grate on Dave. As I mentioned earlier, one example is that he is ill at ease telling a fellow professional, such as a director of photography or a score composer, that his work is not up to snuff. Needless to say, no matter how good these professionals are, this happens a fair bit. Although, in Dave's perfect world, everyone working on his films would have the title "assistant storyteller", unfortunately, this being the real world, what frequently happens is that the composer, say, will produce a piece of music that he loves but that does not serve the story at all. At this point, someone has to confront the composer and break the news that a rewrite is in order.

In these instances, this someone can be only Dave—the composer, rightly, wouldn't listen to anyone other than the director. So, to combat his dislike of this kind of confrontation, Dave appeals to what he calls "the third person in the room: the god of art." Confrontation for confrontation's sake weakens him, but confrontation for the sake of producing higher-quality art? This brings him strength. So, whenever circumstances force these kinds of conflicts, he conjures in his mind's eye what the god of art would want. Thus fortified, he calls the composer in and confronts him for the sake of better art.

• • •

Quit the role, tweak the role, seek out the right partners, or find an aspect of the role that brings you strength: these four tactics will prove the most effective as you strive to smooth away the irritants from your strengths' path. Such are the pressures in today's working world—frequent change, undermanned teams in downsized companies, well-meaning bosses, the widespread belief that well-roundedness equals effectiveness—that, although armed with these tactics, you may not find it easy to stay on this path. And even if you can withstand these pressures, there may be stretches in your career where you deliberately deviate from your strengths' path in the hope that the diversion will lead to better things further on.

To fortify you against these pressures, and to inject a motivating dose of reality into your hopeful diversions, keep mindful of this essential principle: the longer you put up with aspects of your work you don't like, the less successful you will be. So, as far as you are able, and as quickly as you can, stop doing them, and then see what the best of you, now focused and unfettered, can achieve.

# CONCLUSION

# Intentional Imbalance

A long time ago, in a galaxy far, far away, two of the most eminent programmers in the Universe, Fook and Lunkwill, turned on Deep Thought, the supercomputer they had built, composed themselves, and leaned in to ask their question.

"O Deep Thought computer," Fook said. (At least I think it was Fook who actually posed the question. I am relying on Douglas Adams's book *The Hitchhiker's Guide to the Galaxy* as my primary source material for this.) "The task we have designed you to perform is this. We want you to tell us . . . the Answer!"

"The Answer?" said Deep Thought. "The Answer to what?"

"Life!" urged Fook.

"The Universe!" said Lunkwill.

"Everything!" they said in chorus.

It took Deep Thought more than seven million years to compute the answer, but unfortunately, when he revealed it to the assembled multitudes, it proved to be possibly the least illuminating answer anyone had ever heard. According to Deep Thought, the Answer to Life, the Universe, and Everything was "forty-two".

If you've read *The Hitchhiker's Guide to the Galaxy,* you'll recognize this for what it is: Douglas Adams poking fun at anyone trying to find the one Answer. If you go searching for it, his story warns us, you may wind up looking as daft as Deep Thought.

Nonetheless, over the centuries, a few decidedly nondaft people have set out to try. René Descartes was one. After months spent contemplating the passersby on the street beneath his upstairs bedroom, he landed on "I think, therefore I am" as his one Answer. Albert Einstein was another. Having completed his special and general theories of relativity, he then devoted the last twenty-five years of his life to discovering an all-encompassing theory that could reconcile the two. More recently, the eminent theoretical physicist Stephen Hawking published a book titled *The Theory of Everything* in which he described his quest for a theory that could explain, well, everything, from the expansion of the universe to the interaction of minuscule particles called quarks. And Hawking, although something of an iconoclast, is not alone in this quest. Here's another physicist, the Nobel laureate Leon Lederman, expressing a hope that is apparently shared by much of the scientific community: "My ambition is to live to see all of physics reduced to a formula so elegant and simple that it will fit easily on the front of a T-shirt."

All evidence suggests that, despite the warnings of satirists such as Douglas Adams, something in our DNA makes us yearn for short, clear answers to complex problems.

Yes, these cravings may occasionally lead us to give credence to overly simplistic, reductionistic conclusions, some of which, such as that the earth is flat or that skin colour determines intelligence, almost approach the absurdity of "forty-two".

However, on a deeper level, we can see that these cravings for clear answers serve a vital function. Back during our prehistory those of us who were able to come to clear conclusions and to act quickly on these conclusions—Are you friend or foe? Do I eat you or do you eat me?—were more likely to survive than those of us who, confused by the world's complexity, dithered and dallied. Today, these cravings prove equally powerful. Properly channeled, they enable us to pierce complexity and to identify the single best vantage point from which to examine this complexity, make it clear, and take decisive action. They push us to find a perspective, a point of view, that will distinguish between those things that can be ignored and those that demand our attention.

Our effort in this book has been to reveal a few of these perspectives, or, stated differently, to satisfy these cravings for clear insight while avoiding their more simplistic excesses.

We've delved into three multifaceted subjects—managing, leading, and sustained individual success—and have withstood, I hope, the temptation to land on one answer, one step, or one action that drives excellence. Instead we've found three controlling insights, three perspectives, that will serve you well as you strive to find success and satisfaction in this complex world of competing interests.

To excel as a manager you must never forget that each of your direct reports is unique and that your chief responsibility is not to eradicate this uniqueness, but rather to arrange roles, responsibilities, and expectations so that you can capitalize upon it. The more you perfect this skill, the more effectively you will turn talents into performance.

To excel as a leader requires the opposite skill. You must become adept at calling upon those needs we all share. Our common needs include the need for security, for community, for authority, and for respect, but, for you, the leader, the most powerful universal need is our need for clarity. To transform our fear of the unknown into confidence in the future, you must discipline yourself to describe our joint future vividly and precisely. As your skill at this grows, so will our confidence in you.

And last, you must remember that your sustained success depends on your ability to cut out of your working life those activities, or people, that pull you off your strengths' path. Your leader can show you clearly your better future. Your manager can draft you on to the team and cast you into the right role on the team. However, it will always be *your* responsibility to make the small but significant course corrections that allow you to sustain your highest and best contribution to this team, and to the better future it is charged with creating. The more skilled you are at this, the more valued, and fulfilled, and successful you will become.

As we've seen in each of these roles, the critical skill is not balance, but its inverse, intentional imbalance. The great manager bets that he will prevail by magnifying, emphasizing, and then capitalizing on each employee's uniqueness. The great leader comes to a conclusion about his core customer, his organization's strength, its core score, and the actions he will commit to right now, and then, in the service of clarity, banishes from his thought and conversation almost everything else. The sustainably effective individual, by rigorously removing the irritants from his working life, engages with the world in an equally imbalanced fashion.

It takes insight to focus in this way, and discipline, and since lopsided bets can be scary, courage. My hope for this book is that it has served to strengthen in you all three.

• • •

To learn more about *The One Thing You Need to Know,* please visit marcusbuckingham.com.

# Acknowledgments

This book required liberal quantities of faith from many smart people who are not normally given to taking such leaps.

Joni Evans was one. Why she was so certain that things would work out for the best I have no idea, but she did, and they have, and I am deeply in her debt.

Fred Hills was another. He made a big play early on, and then during the long months of research and writing, he never displayed any doubt about the outcome. His confidence was contagious, and so now we have a book. Kirsa Rein, thank you for keeping him in line.

Linda and Mitch Hart, although rational and wise in most every other respect, proved to be almost unreasonably optimistic when it came to this project. Indeed, their optimism seemed to exist in inverse proportion to my own worries. On this quality I relied heavily.

Barry Haldeman also shouldered much of the burden of this book. He saw a path when I did not, and inched us along it, one calm conversation at a time. Harley Neuman, too, with his competence, his good heart, and his resolve, owns a piece of this.

So does the team of leaders at the Free Press: Carolyn

Reidy; Martha Levin; Suzanne Donahue; Dominick Anfuso; Carisa Hays; and Michele Jacob. They serve as an example of how things should be done.

And then there were the early readers. Ben Sherwood and Tiffany Ward responded to the first couple of chapters with insight, intelligence, and above all, diplomacy. Thank you both for being so deft.

Friends listened patiently and politely as I threw ill-formed ideas at them in lieu of proper conversation. The U.S. contingent: John and Laura; Tim and Sarah; Mark and Julie; Steve and Andrea; Richard and Andrea; Ben and Jen; Judi and Gotham; Dave and Melissa; Elliot; and, as ever, Nader and Ingrid. The long-suffering U.K. contingent: Mike, Miles and Steve; Tim and Penny; Luly and Pete; Alex and Pod; Charles and Vic. Thank you for returning my calls.

Many people allowed me into their lives and trusted me with their stories. I learned a great deal from each of them, and have tried to capture these lessons in the book. Thank you Judi, Carrie, Dave, Myrtle, Tim, Andy, Keric, Catherine, Tami, Preston, Chris, Russ, Manjit, Michelle, Jim, Melissa, Terry, David, Brad, and Steve.

And to my Gallup family, a bow to the great work you do. Kelly, Brian, Dana, Steve, Charles, Guido, Don B., Jim H., Warren, Tom, and of course, Jan. And to Jim and Larry, thank you for your energy and focus these many years.

We all need fellow travellers to reassure us that our journey is worthwhile. Tony Schwarz is mine. Thank you for the companionship.

Emma Cunningham is so ridiculously good at her job, I am

at a loss as to what to say about her. If you call me, you'll get her, and then you'll know what I mean.

Mum, Dad, Nelly, and Pips, le tout famille Buckingham, bear most of the responsibility for getting me to where I am today in one piece. I owe them pretty much everything.

Don, I miss you. Thank you for your life and your legacy.

Janie, I love you.

And Jackson and Lilia? Well, the One Thing I know for sure is that I wish I had met you both sooner.

# About the Author

Marcus Buckingham graduated from Cambridge University in 1987, with a master's degree in social and political science. During his seventeen years with The Gallup Organization, Buckingham helped lead research into the world's best leaders, managers, and workplaces. This research formed the basis for two bestselling books: *First, Break All the Rules: What the World's Best Managers Do Differently* and *Now, Discover Your Strengths*.

A subject of in-depth profiles in the *Sunday Telegraph*, the *New York Times, Fortune,* and *Fast Company,* Buckingham, now an independent consultant, author and speaker, is considered one of the world's leading authorities on employee productivity and the practices of leading and managing. He is a member of the secretary of state's Advisory Committee on Leadership and Management. He lives with his wife and two children in Los Angeles.